m
mettle

BIBLE READING NOTES

TO INSPIRE
COURAGE SPIRIT CHARACTER

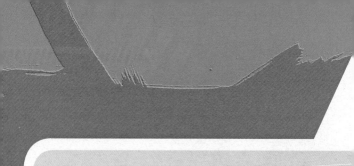

Copyright © YFC and CWR 2008

Published 2008 by CWR, Waverley Abbey House, Waverley Lane, Farnham, Surrey GU9 8EP, England.

Mettle Bible reading notes are produced in association with British Youth for Christ. British Youth for Christ is part of Youth for Christ International, a movement of youth evangelism organisations in over 100 countries of the world. Please visit www.yfci.org for the country nearest you.

Series Editors: Gavin Calver, Phil Sheldrake and Lorne Campbell
Contributors: Jo White, Phil Sheldrake, Steve Warner, Simon Mills (writing on behalf of Open Doors, UK)

See back of book for list of National Distributors.

Unless otherwise indicated, all Scripture references are from the Holy Bible, New Living Translation (NLT), copyright © 1996, revised 2004. Used by permission of Tyndale House Publishers, Inc., Wheaton, Illinois 60189. All rights reserved.

Concept development by YFC and CWR.

Editing design and production by CWR.

Printed in England by Linney Print.

CONTENTS

WELCOME TO

mettle COURAGE SPIRIT CHARACTER ...

Welcome to *Mettle*! Well, what's in this issue?

'The end is near!' Have you ever heard that statement? Let's face it, we may occasionally worry, but quickly push the scary thoughts from our mind. So in our core theme we'll consider the 'End Times' – from Jesus' promise to return to God's final judgment and eternal life.

In our 'Hot Potatoes' we'll be looking at leading, living and obeying. First up – 'Leading'. We hope to inspire confidence in you and challenge you to lead, and serve, your friends. Then, 'Living'.

The world tells us to become go-getting, jet-setting, walking-talking successes, but is that really *living*? Finally, 'Obeying'. We all follow rules and social conventions – wearing school uniform, sticking to the speed limit or even buying the 'right' brands. Here we'll examine what Bible characters learnt about following rules.

We'd love to hear your thoughts about *Mettle*, so do email them to us at mettle@yfc.co.uk. Well, that said, let's get in!

The *Mettle* Team

END TIMES

Welcome to our study on the 'End Times'.

I've been a Christian for almost twenty years now and, to my shame, I've not spent much time considering what the 'End Times' will be like – despite believing that at some point this world will be changed and renewed. It's easier not to bother considering the subject because it seems ages away and doesn't appear to affect us personally. Add this to the fact that understanding what the Bible says about the 'End Times' can be challenging, I find that thinking about the 'End Times' is rarely at the top of my priority list!

'No eye has seen, no ear has heard, and no mind has imagined what God has prepared for those who love him.' KEY VERSE v9

Even heavy-weight theologians get stumped by the books of Revelation and Daniel. However, flicking through the Bible, I realised that not a page goes by without some evidence of the divine stopwatch ticking down to zero hour. There will actually be an end to this world, as we know it. It cannot go on forever like this. God has shown us what will eventually happen, and so we need to take some time to try to understand this.

Today's verse encourages us that with the help of the Holy Spirit, we can grasp something of the mind of God about these things. So what does the Bible say about the 'End Times'? What does it all mean for us and how do we handle it? We'll be looking at these questions and more, as we investigate what the Bible reveals.

PRAY

Lord God, there's lots of fear surrounding the 'End Times' and what will happen. Please reveal Your truth about Your plans – and where times, dates and facts are Your concern, help me to trust that You have everything under control. Amen.

'When the Spirit of truth comes, he will guide you into all truth ... He will tell you about the future.'

KEY VERSE
v13

FRI 2 MAY

6

THINK

Whether we are nearer the end than the beginning of the 'End Times' remains to be seen, yet we can safely say that we are living in them. This means that it would be crazy to ignore what the Bible tells us about this point in our world's history.

The study of the 'End Times' (or 'eschatology' if you want to impress) is quite simply the study of what the Bible says is 'yet to come'. Included within this topic is Jesus' promise to return to earth, what will happen to this world, God's final judgment and eternal life. In Parts One and Two, we'll consider firstly general aspects of the 'End Times', then take a closer look at some 'landmarks' (key features). These are open to various interpretations by Bible scholars, but we'll try to discover a few pointers to help us understand the language and imagery used.

Later on we'll analyse what Jesus personally said about the 'End Times' and the kingdom of God – and lastly we'll discover what we're meant to do about it all.

Often the first question people ask is, 'Are we actually living in the "End Times"?' The short answer is 'Yes'. Jesus' death and resurrection marked the beginning of these 'last days'. Jesus' return to heaven and the gift of the Holy Spirit, described in today's passage, indicate that we are now waiting for Jesus to return once more to bring an end to this current age.

KEY VERSE
v1

'Don't let your hearts be troubled. Trust in God, and trust also in me.'

It can be really confusing when people are talking about the 'End Times' and start using words and phrases that seem weird. So here's a brief rundown of some of the terms we might come across when reading about the 'End Times'.

The Rapture = used to describe the moment when Christians (dead or alive) get taken up to be with Jesus.

The Tribulation = a terrible time of suffering that will occur around the time Jesus comes again.

Second Coming = when Jesus comes again to earth as Judge and King

Judgment Seat of Christ = a big throne occupied by Jesus when He's judging the whole earth.

Antichrist = evil personified into a man (often thought to be a political/world leader) who appears on the earth to deceive many by claiming that he is God.

CONTINUED ▶

The Beast = another name for Satan, describing his destructive nature.

Dragon = another picture used to portray Satan.

New Jerusalem = God's own replacement city that will appear from heaven but come down to earth. Christians will live here after Jesus has come again.

Eternal Life = the gift that all Christians receive when they believe that Jesus died and rose again for them in payment for all the sins they have committed.

Millennium = a period of a thousand years when some Christians believe that Jesus is going to reign on earth after He returns for the second and final time.

Apocalypse = derives from the Greek word meaning 'unveiling' or 'revealing'

Don't be afraid to ask questions to find out what things mean.

PRAY

Father, help me to have the confidence to ask others about things I don't understand. Challenge me to find out more and not to just ignore what will happen. Thank You that my future is safe in You and that You will ultimately bring understanding. Amen.

KEY VERSE v9

'He does not want anyone to be destroyed, but wants everyone to repent.'

The big finale of this current age will be the return of Jesus to earth; His *second coming*. Only then will the world truly realise who has been behind the scenes of this universe. However, even in Peter's day, there were many who began to doubt that Jesus would ever come back.

When watching the news or browsing the internet, it can be easy to lose sight of Jesus' promise to return. We might find ourselves joining in with those mentioned in today's passage who questioned whether Jesus would keep His promise. Life may continue and everything may seem to go on as it always has since the beginning of creation. However, we need never doubt Jesus' promise to return, because the Bible clearly shows us that God does not go back on His Word or break a promise.

As Peter explains, Jesus is being patient and merciful by delaying His return, in order that many more people may come to know Him. But when He does return, everyone is going to know about it, as the Lord appears in glory in the skies around the entire world!

MON 5 MAY 9

PRAY

Take a moment to thank God that He keeps His promises. Think of a time in your life where God has been faithful to you and give Him some more thanks! Now thank God that He is coming back to claim you as His own forever.

'I am the Alpha and the Omega, the First and the Last, the Beginning and the End.'

KEY VERSE
v13

THINK

Did you know that you are a precious part of God's plan in the world's timeline? Spend a moment thinking about how awesome it is to be known by God.

Yesterday, we learnt that God keeps His promises, but there is also further evidence that backs up Jesus' promise to return. In creating the world, God created the concept of time through creating both the sun (sunrise and sunset) and the moon. This introduced the concept of a beginning and therefore of an end.

In today's passage, Jesus describes Himself as both the Beginning and the End because He was and will be present at both world events. In John 1:1–2 we read that, *'In the beginning the Word already existed. The Word was with God and the Word was God. He existed in the beginning with God.'* And in Revelation 19:11 we see a visual picture of Jesus as the Judge of the world riding on a white horse on that last day.

With this in mind, we can see that God has given the world a timeline and planned out what will happen to His creation. The idea that God has the complete picture in view is both mind-blowing and comforting. To know that this same God also sees our lives, loves us and wants to know us can be hard to grasp, yet we can be reassured that we are a key part of His plan.

KEY VERSE v23

'... he sent Adam out to cultivate the ground from which he had been made.'

You may be wondering why today's reading is from Genesis rather than Revelation. Sometimes, taking another look at the beginning helps us to understand more about the end. The Garden of Eden, as described in chapter 2 of Genesis, provides a picture of what eternal life on the new Earth (Revelation 21:1) might be like in the future.

Prior to Adam and Eve sinning, life was intended to go on forever – through mankind eating the fruit from the tree of life. However, with the introduction of sin through Adam and Eve, God could not allow us to live forever. He was therefore forced to banish humanity from the Garden of Eden – bringing death and isolation from God to mankind.

Revelation 22:2 shows a picture of two trees of life growing within the New Jerusalem. Someday these trees of life will be available for all of God's people to eat from. Ultimately, we learn from Revelation and other teaching about the 'End Times' that God desires to restore life in all its fullness to mankind.

WED 7 MAY

11

Do you have a picture in your mind of what an ideal world would look like? Expand that picture by reading Revelation 21 for inspiration.

THINK

READING: 1 Corinthians 15:1–23

'Christ was raised as the first of the harvest; then all who belong to Christ will be raised when he comes back.'

KEY VERSE
v23

THURS 8 MAY

12

PRAY

Ask God to help you grasp how awesome Jesus is and to reveal to you more about the hope that we have of eternal life.

Not only was Jesus' life the turning point in God's plan for all humanity, but it became the pivotal point of world history. This is illustrated by the way in which historians introduced a dating system revolving around His birth (BC/AD). This also demonstrates just how important it is to understand the significance of Jesus' life, if we are to be clear about the End Times.

Grasping the relevance of Jesus' death and resurrection helps us appreciate what will happen at the end of this current age. It is His resurrection, in particular, that gives us an indication of what to expect for *ourselves*. If you believe in Jesus, you are now part of the kingdom of God and are able to gain eternal life because of Christ's own resurrection. Without the prospect of experiencing resurrection at the end of the age, there would be no hope for us and our faith would all have been a waste of time!

However, because Jesus has gone ahead of us and experienced resurrection, we can be sure that God will also resurrect us who have died prior to Jesus' second coming – and this time we'll live with Him for eternity.

KEY VERSE v23

'For the wages of sin is death, but the free gift of God is eternal life through Christ Jesus our Lord.'

The one thing I couldn't help noticing when reading about the 'End Times' is the way in which the choice between eternal life and eternal death is so clear cut. In fact, it forced me to have a good look at my own faith; whether or not I had been living with that choice at the very heart of *my* thinking.

It's easy to be casual in our attitude to heaven and hell, yet the hard truth is that Christians believe that after this life we do go to one or the other.

The End Times force us to make two choices. The first one is between the kingdom of heaven and hell: 'Where am I going?' And the second is between keeping quiet or telling others: 'What does living in the End Times mean for the way I tell others about Jesus?'

Jesus' return is getting nearer – and there is now a greater urgency than ever to communicate to others the need for them to make a decision (one way or another) about Jesus.

FRI 9 MAY

13

CHALLENGE

Have you made that first choice to commit your whole life to following Jesus? If not, talk to your youth leader or a Christian friend. If you have, then write down two ways that you'll begin to tell others about their need to make a decision.

KEY VERSE
v40

'Two men will be working together in the field; one will be taken, the other left.'

Despite controversy amongst Bible scholars, there are a number of interesting features of the End Times worth studying more closely. We'll look at six of them this week, starting today with the idea of the *Rapture*.

There'll always be disagreement about when exactly this will happen and how it will take place. Some scholars also argue that parts of this prophetic passage were fulfilled in AD 70, when the Roman army destroyed Jerusalem and the Temple.

One Christian viewpoint is that Jesus is describing an event where men and women will suddenly be taken from the earth, leaving behind others who, it is assumed, are those who don't believe. This indicates that the Rapture will be sudden and will catch people unawares.

Verses 16 and 17 of 1 Thessalonians 4 also indicate that believers will be taken up to meet the Lord in the air in a way similar to the Lord's departure from earth after His resurrection. Reading on into chapter 5, you'll see that the event is described as coming 'like a thief in the night' but, as 'children of the light' (v.5), believers should not be concerned since they belong to Jesus. All of this may be figurative language, not to be taken literally (and may have had a different meaning to first-century Jewish Christians), but one thing is clear – Jesus will return suddenly, so we must live our lives as if we expect Him to return at any time.

THINK

As believers, we should be living as faithful and sensible servants of Jesus, actively expecting Him to return for us at any moment. We should therefore keep a short account of sin in our lives, bringing it to Jesus for forgiveness.

'Then there will be a time of anguish greater than any since nations first came into existence.'

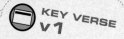

KEY VERSE
V1

THINK

MON 12 MAY

16

What's your view about the *Tribulation*? Why not read up on it or chat with your church leaders. They may recommend some good reading material for you to begin your study.

The second End Times landmark is called the *Tribulation*. This is a period of great global suffering, referred to in the Bible as the 'time of God's wrath', when He pours out judgments similar to but worse than those experienced by Egypt in the time of Moses.

Just like the *Rapture* (which not everyone takes literally), there's lot of discussion about when the *Tribulation* occurs. Some believe it will happen before the *Rapture*, meaning that both Christians and non-Christians will face suffering together. Others believe that Christians will only endure until halfway through, being raptured and leaving behind non-believers to face an even greater tribulation. However, there are still others who say that the Tribulation occurs after the Rapture, due to Bible references about God rescuing His people from suffering (Rev. 3:10).

Whatever your take – and it's worth having one! – it's clear that the Tribulation is a period of time where God's anger at the world is unleashed. Yet, we have the reassurance that we're saved by Jesus and will be with Him at the end, regardless of what suffering we endure now or later.

KEY VERSE
v3

'For that day will not come until there is a great rebellion against God and the man of lawlessness is revealed ...'

The world seems to contain some crazy leaders. Some are in charge of countries and doing really awful things. Many of these modern-day world leaders (just like leaders in previous centuries) have at some point been considered to be the 'Antichrist' – which is our third landmark on the journey to understanding the End Times.

Whilst each of them may have shared similar characteristics with the Antichrist (pride, control or arrogance), it is impossible for us to know when and where the actual Antichrist (as described in the poetic, symbolic language of Daniel and Revelation) will appear. The Antichrist is also described in detail in today's passage as a man who'll accomplish great evil, being possessed by the devil. He will be full of lies, deceit and – in the book of Daniel – is described as a world ruler; a king who conquers many countries.

The Antichrist will be evil personified (a perfect example of evil) and some believe that he will be the final ruler on earth before Jesus returns, even claiming to be God! Christians are urged to be watchful – but we need not fear such evil, for Jesus is described as destroying the Antichrist with His very breath and the splendour of His second coming!

TUES 13 MAY

17

You do not need to fear! Isn't that amazing? God is in total control of world events, no matter who rises to power or how evil someone is.

THINK

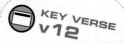

'And the dead were judged according to what they had done, as recorded in the books.'

KEY VERSE
v12

THINK

Do you believe that God's judgments are just and true? If not, think about what the world would look like without them. Read Psalm 58:10–11 for more food for thought.

There's a whole lot a judgment going on in the book of Revelation – which is a book of pictorial, symbolic language and is pretty hard for us to understand! With all the terrible earthquakes listed, the rivers and sea turning to blood, the poisonous locusts and scorching sun, you'd be forgiven for wanting to turn on the telly rather than read on through.

Our fourth landmark of the End Times is God's judgment. The Bible describes the End Times as full of God's wrath. We've already learnt about the Tribulation; however the Tribulation is also broken up into a series of specific judgments under the headings of 'Seals', 'Trumpets' and 'Bowls', all of which seem to increase in nastiness, arriving at the final day of judgment when God the Father judges all.

Because of the evil within the world, God's judgment is necessary in order to put an end to sin once and for all. We can be confident that God is a just and true Judge, who won't be deceived or manipulated by humanity, but will judge rightly and fairly. Therefore, we can look forward to this day when everyone will see that the Lord is King over all.

KEY VERSE
v7

'Let us be glad and rejoice ... For the time has come for the wedding feast of the Lamb ...'

Our fifth landmark of the End Times is the amazing celebration of Jesus' victory over death. Once and for all, Satan will be destroyed and we will be able to join in the biggest party in the history of the universe. In Revelation, the picture that's used to describe this event is a wedding banquet, where Jesus is the bridegroom and His Church is the bride.

If you've ever been to a wedding as a guest, you'll know how incredible they can be – with everyone dressed in their finest clothes, a huge three-course meal for the guests and a massive cake. However, when you're the bride or groom, the intensity of the experience goes up a few notches and you can get totally overwhelmed by the excitement and energy of the party!

After our wedding day, my husband and I took three whole days to come down off the adrenaline buzz! I can only dream of what it might be like at the wedding of Christ to His Church. It will be the final party to beat all parties! Plus there's the added bonus that the cake in heaven will be everyone's favourite flavour!

THURS 15 MAY

19

CHALLENGE

Encourage your youth group or Christian mates to hold a party and invite your non-Christian friends. Then, why not give a short talk or presentation to them about what it's like to actually know Jesus; especially in the days in which we're now living.

'They all came to life again, and they reigned with Christ for a thousand years.'

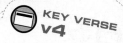 KEY VERSE v4

THINK

Have your questions about the End Times been answered in Part One? If not, ask your youth leader or pastor for more information. Don't be afraid to ask for recommended reading too! It's good to read around what is a much talked-about topic.

The final landmark we'll look at this week is the period of one thousand years or the *Millennium*, as it is frequently called. From what John tells us in Revelation (remember – a book full of pictorial language and symbolism), this period will be free from the devil's tyranny, as he'll be under the lock and key of a heavyweight angel. This means that there'll be no deception or sin during this time and, furthermore, believers who have died for their faith will have the opportunity to reign with Jesus.

Some scholars believe that the Millennium and the final judgment form the last chapter of earth's history before a new earth and heaven are brought into place and we enter into the ages to come; eternal life with Christ. Other respected Christian scholars, however, would interpret the teaching on the Millennium in a completely different way. It's a big subject!

We've looked at some of the more discussed features of the End Times this week, but there are plenty more to read about. Why not try to find some more before we return to this topic later on in the summer?

KEY VERSE v12

'Don't let anyone think less of you because you are young. Be an example to all believers in what you say ...'

LEADING

Welcome to our two-part look at *Leading*. Over these two sections, we're going to be examining the characteristics of being a leader: what leadership is and what it is not. What can we learn from the way Jesus led? How can we lead our friends whilst at the same time serving them? How can we support our leaders? And how can we develop the wisdom and the perseverance to lead?

This whole section isn't about becoming the next prime minister or being employed as the CEO of a multi-million pound organisation. You can be a leader at school – someone other people look up to, respect and follow. You can be a leader at work, whatever job you do. Other staff will look to you and your supervisors will

CONTINUED ▸▸

trust you and give you responsibility. Being a leader is about leading people in a good and beneficial way.

In the movie, *Kingdom of Heaven*, Balian (the blacksmith who becomes a knight and later the defender of Jerusalem) lives by the motto: *'What man is a man who does not make the world better?'*

As Christians, is this why we are here? To make the world a better place? Is that all? There must be more to it than that! We must ask the question *'How can God's will be done on earth as it is in heaven?'* Are you willing to be a part of the answer?

THINK

Jesus commanded us to go into the entire world, make disciples and teach them. We're always teaching about Jesus, whether we realise it or not, simply by the way we live and the example we give. The question is: What kind of Jesus are we teaching people about?

'And a voice from heaven said, "This is my dearly loved Son, who brings me great joy."'

Part of being a leader is knowing who you are. This is central to where you're going, what your calling is and your identity. To be strong and courageous, wise and influential, an example and a friend to others, you need to know who *you* are.

Who you are is not what you do, who you work with or who you hang around with – or even who you're related to. The people you are with and the things you do change over time, but you cannot simply change as these external factors shift.

Your true identity is found in being rooted in God. Recognising that you are created in the image of God, are following Jesus and are being continually filled with the Holy Spirit is essential. You can be secure in the fact that you are now rooted in God and are not measured by how much you produce or achieve. What a huge relief! The pressure's off! If achievement and success define you, then you'll always be chasing after them – like chasing the wind.

Jesus had not begun any sort of ministry when the Father in heaven said that He loved Him and that He was already pleased with Him. Jesus had nothing to prove!

MON 19 MAY

23

THINK

What defines you? Identity is such a huge and complicated issue but you can start by reading the Bible and discovering what God says about you. Friends may change, schools and jobs come and go, but God's truth remains true at all times.

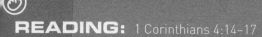
'So I urge you to imitate me.'

KEY VERSE
v16

TUES 20 MAY

24

THINK

Who are you following and why do you follow them? Who is following you? Are you setting them a good example?

Leadership is a funny thing. You can think of yourself as a leader, read books about being a leader, go to seminars on being a leader and have a plaque on an office door saying you're a leader, but if no one else recognises that then what's the point? Leaders need people to follow them – need to have people who want to be led – otherwise, well, they're not leading anyone!

Developing the quality of leadership is about firstly recognising that you yourself are following someone else. The apostle Paul says in 1 Corinthians 11:1, 'And you should imitate me, just as I imitate Christ.' Just because you may not literally be at the top of an organisation, youth group or football team, it does not mean that you're not leading. As you follow Christ and seek to imitate Him, you begin to develop leadership qualities.

Whether you're 'Top Dog', or not, doesn't matter. To be a good leader, what does matter is the ability to recognise a good leadership example and to lead as you yourself are led. What better example of this than Jesus!

KEY VERSE
v17

'Dear brothers and sisters, pattern your lives after mine, and learn from those who follow our example.'

Another funny thing about leadership is that people often consider themselves a leader when the title of leader is suddenly bestowed upon them. You might know people like this: those who've suddenly been given the job of leader (in being made captain of the football team or House Captain at school, for example). However, they don't seem to know what to do with the title because their eyes are still fixed on their own leader, who they are looking up to.

Although the dictionary says that *leadership* is a noun, in practice it's more like a verb. It's a doing word! Leadership is all about *what* we do, *how* we do it and *why* we do it. If you want to be a leader, then learn from other leaders. Then, at the right time, start giving people a reason to follow your lead. People need to believe in a leader as well as a cause. Strong leadership is essential!

The first name for Christianity in the Early Church was *The Way*, because people were following *The Way* that Jesus showed them to live.

WED 21 MAY

25

CHALLENGE

Christian leadership is all about example – showing people a way to *The Way*. In what way are people following you? What patterns are they learning from you? Are these patterns good or bad? Do you need to reexamine your leadership style? Is it Christlike?

'He does only what he sees the Father doing. Whatever the Father does, the Son also does.'

THURS 22 MAY

26

THINK

Do you represent an organisation, a team or a youth group? If so, how? Do you lead strongly, so that others recognise the authority given to you by your organisation? Have you ever thought about how you represent the kingdom of God to others? Does your leading point to a greater power – Jesus Christ?

There's a curious story of Jesus encountering a Roman officer whose servant is sick. The officer displays an amazing understanding of faith in Jesus' authority. So much so, that Jesus commends him as an example to the Jewish crowds, who themselves were supposedly the people of God. They, not this Roman soldier, should have been able to recognise Jesus' authority!

The Roman officer, with perhaps no knowledge of Israel's history or of Jesus' being the Messiah, said: 'Lord, I am not worthy to have you come into my home. Just say the word from where you are, and my servant will be healed. I know this because I am under the authority of my superior officers, and I have authority over my soldiers. I only need to say, "Go" and they go, or "Come," and they come. And if I say to my slaves, "Do this," they do it' (Matt. 8:8–9).

Jesus was amazed at his response. It showed a clear understanding of Jesus' leadership authority: He represented the kingdom of heaven on earth and had authority (from the Father) over both life and death.

KEY VERSE v15

'I have given you an example to follow. Do as I have done to you.'

This example of Jesus' *servant leadership* will often be quoted at some point by Christians teaching us about leading. As leaders, no matter what sphere of influence we have, who we're in charge of or even the responsibilities we have, this example of servanthood is the best way to lead people.

However, being a servant cuts two ways. Some leaders get put upon by those they serve, because their style of leadership is considered by others as weak. Jesus, on the other hand, demonstrates meekness – a word which here means having power under control.

What is the difference? Jesus is completely secure in His role as leader and teacher – the way in which He speaks could even be mistaken for arrogance if we did not know His character better. He leads by example and directs His followers to do as He does: *'Do as I have done to you.'*

While He was on earth, there was no 'putting upon' Jesus. He didn't get walked over. He didn't seek others' approval, because the only approval He needed was that of His heavenly Father. This was where He drew His security.

FRI 23 MAY

27

PRAY

Thank You, Father, that the only approval I need to lead in a godly way is Yours. Help me not to run after human approval as I seek – in Your strength – to develop my leadership abilities.

KEY VERSE
v45

'For even the Son of Man came not to be served but to serve others and to give his life as a ransom for many.'

In 2005, three Indonesian ladies, Rebekka, Eti and Ratna, were imprisoned for running a Sunday School in their local community. They were accused of trying to convert Muslim children to Christianity – a serious crime against Islam. On entering prison they proceeded to serve both the inmates and the guards. Rebekka, a qualified doctor, tended the sick and the other ladies regularly cleaned up the place. All three women served with poise, grace, humility and a dignity that won over their fellow prisoners. Eventually, they were even allowed to hold their own church services within the prison and people came to follow their example by following Christ themselves!

Early in 2007, Rebekka, Eti and Ratna were set free. It was an emotional time for the prison, as these ladies had made an indelible impact on people through their Christ-like service. Through servant leadership, they became people of respect and influence within the prison.

This is the quality of leading Jesus passed on to His disciples when they began to get ideas above their station! Leadership is about example and demonstration. If your example is to boss people around so that they achieve your goals, then how will these people treat you when they become disillusioned and fed up with your style? Certainly not with respect!

Instead, our Christlike style of leadership is supposed to demonstrate the kingdom and its values – which often appear a little topsy-turvy compared to our world's values. So, why not be the first, the pioneer, the ground-breaker, by leading your mates in the way of servant leadership?

CHALLENGE

How can I serve the Persecuted Church? How can I make a difference?

Why not talk to one of your leaders, asking what your church is doing or is willing to do and how you can get involved?

READING: 1 Peter 5:1–6

'In the same way, you younger men must accept the authority of the elders. And all of you, serve each other in humility ...'

KEY VERSE v5

MON 26 MAY

30

THINK

What does leadership really mean to you? Is it telling people what to do? Is that the kind of leader you aspire to be? Or is leadership about influencing others for their benefit?

Whenever God teaches us a truth about leadership, it's possible, of course, for people to twist and misuse it. For example, we could see the idea of humbling ourselves for a little while as a kind of magic formula whereby God will then give us amazing blessings afterwards, as a reward: *'If I put myself at the bottom then God will put me at the top!'*

Servant leadership is not about what we'll *eventually* get out of a situation. It's about serving no matter *what* and no matter *who* right up until the day we die.

Peter is talking to us, as the Church, about respecting the authority of those in leadership over us; putting ourselves under their authority with humility. By respecting those above us – even if we don't always agree with them – we slowly learn the art of leadership, through obedience and humility.

If you want to be a leader, respect, obedience and humility are character traits you'll have to develop, ready for when, if it's God's will, it's your turn to lead. Rather than simply reading a quick 'How to ...' guide on leading, you may need to learn from other leaders (parents, teachers, etc), by submitting to their authority already in your life.

KEY VERSE v1

'This is a trustworthy saying: "If someone aspires to be an elder, he desires an honorable position."'

Some people say that true leaders are born to lead, whilst others say that leaders can be trained. The fact is that both statements are true. Winston Churchill was one of the greatest leaders Britain has ever known. During the worst circumstances, he came to power leading the United Kingdom from potential defeat to victory in World War II.

Churchill is famous for his rousing spirit expressed in stirring speeches, but he was also known as an audacious, even arrogant, person; full of self-belief that he should lead. Before World War II, he was a mediocre politician without much of a track record for success in politics. After World War II, his political career rested much upon his fame for leading the United Kingdom through the war to victory.

He said this of himself: *I felt as if I were walking with destiny, and that all my past life had been but a preparation for this hour and this trial.*

It is said that 'calling' is where the greatest passion meets the world's greatest need. This was Churchill's moment and he led with courage, perseverance, strength and character, being quoted as saying, *'Never, never, never give up'*.

TUES 27 MAY

31

THINK

Does circumstance produce character or does character dictate the circumstance? Are you a leader by nature or is it being nurtured in you? Do you want to be a leader? Can you find those to help you become a leader?

'And so, King Agrippa, I obeyed that vision from heaven.'

KEY VERSE
v19

WED 28 MAY

32

CHALLENGE

Do you have a vision? Can you take people with you to make it happen? Paul's vision was to take the good news of Jesus Christ to the non-Jewish nations (the Gentiles). On the way, he raised up many leaders to help him realise this vision.

Good leaders have vision – that ability to see a goal and head straight for it, taking people with them as they go.

Here we see Paul in Caesarea who, having been in prison for two years, is brought out to speak to King Agrippa who was staying for a few days with Governor Festus. As a person, Paul fascinated them both. They couldn't quite work out why the Jewish leaders had it in for Paul, so they gave him the opportunity to speak about why he had been imprisoned.

A visionary leader is very similar to an architect constructing a building. The architect draws a plan of what the building should look like and communicates this to the builders, in order for them to build it. Likewise a visionary leader sees the broad picture and helps other people to understand this vision so that it can become a reality. Paul had a clear vision of what he was supposed to be doing with the rest of his life; a vision of what the future could hold – a world that would know the truth about Jesus.

KEY VERSE
v11

'We also pray that you will ... have all the endurance and patience you need.'

The whole idea of developing patience is a character trait of every good leader. There is a connection between patience and endurance – persevering to the finish of something. Having a vision is one thing, but seeing it through to completion is another matter entirely!

Moses led the children of Israel out of Egypt to the very borders of the promised land – taking 40 years in the process. As a leader, he had to display tremendous patience with a grumbling and ungrateful people. Of course, they did make it out of Egypt and into the promised land, although Moses did not live to see this. In that chapter of history, the finish was better than the start, as the children of Israel went from being slaves to free people, having their own country.

The slow and patient process of creating racial equality in America has been a subject for many leaders in the 20th century. Martin Luther King, another visionary leader, made it his vision and dream in life to lead others in creating equality. He didn't live to see this come about. There may be dreams you're leading others to fulfil that you'll never see through to the end yourself.

THURS 29 MAY

33

PRAY

Help me, Father to learn patience in leadership; to treat people with humility and respect as I work to achieve my goals and visions. Even if I don't ever realise them, may I look back and know that I was a good leader.

'The crowds searched everywhere for him, and when they finally found him, they begged him not to leave them.'

KEY VERSE
v42

THINK

What do people know you for? Is it for positive or negative things? Are you someone who indulges in gossip or do you defend those being talked about? Do you help people or take advantage of them? How can you positively influence and lead people today?

Influence. In nearly every manual, seminar and DVD teaching series on becoming a great leader, you'll find the key word used is *influence*. The funny, yet observant, quote goes: *'If you're not leading anyone then you're just going for a walk.'* Leadership is not primarily about being first, being the smartest or even being at the top – it is about influence; that ability to teach and release other leaders. You can be called a leader, but in your role you have two choices: a) influence others as a leader or b) be influenced and become a follower.

Jesus had influence. How do we know? Well, people followed! Vast crowds went wherever they heard He was going to be. If He had no influence at all, we would not know about Him today. After all, He inspired the writing of the four Gospels!

Is leadership about fame? No! Dominating others? No! Jesus' influence was a result of serving the least, last and lost in society, and of His radical, counter-cultural teaching. Later on, it was His dying for humanity and His resurrection that influenced the whole of human history.

**KEY VERSE
v2**

'"Everything is meaningless," says the Teacher, "completely meaningless!"'

LIVING

Life: what's it all about? That's a big question. Wondering about where we fit into the world can cause us to lose sleep! There's so much pressure these days to *be* a certain way. The world tells us to be, from an early age, cut-throat, go-getting, money-grabbing, jet-setting, walking-talking successes. However, at the end of the day, we can't help but notice what effect this has on some people: it makes them unhappy. We can so easily forget to stop and ask the deeper questions of life.

How do we *live* in the world, when verses like Romans 12:2 teach us not to copy its ways? Can we be 'salt and light' without losing our faith (we'll look at what this means tomorrow)? 'Are we allowed to enjoy this wonderful world, or should we be spending all day,

CONTINUED ▶

every day trying to spread the good news?

Today's passage introduces the very interesting book of Ecclesiastes. It is part of what Christian scholars call Wisdom Literature. Ecclesiastes, along with other Bible books, such as Proverbs, Psalms, Job and Song of Songs, explores some of life's most perplexing issues – and finds that not all of them have clear solutions! The author of Ecclesiastes observed the world around him and considered its patterns and traditions a meaningless waste of time. Let's go forward together and explore our role as Christians living here on earth.

CHALLENGE

Re-read today's passage. What bits do you agree with? What really frustrates you about the world's systems and patterns? Which parts don't you agree with? Is the writer of Ecclesiastes just having a bad day or has he got a point? Stop and reflect on your own experience of 'living' so far. What things are 'meaningless' to you and what aspects are definitely important?

KEY VERSE
v16

'In the same way, let your good deeds shine out for all to see, so that everyone will praise your heavenly Father.'

OK, so with yesterday's reading from Ecclesiastes in mind, let's explore the whole 'salt and light' thing.

When Jesus sat down on the mountainside and taught His disciples, He gave them God's take on what was meaningful. He made some very deep statements which have come to be known as the Beatitudes. God is concerned for and looks after those who mourn, who are humble, who seek justice, and who are merciful, pure and peace-loving. God blesses you if you are punished for doing right, or if you're mocked, lied about or badly treated because you are a Christian.

The amazing thing about living is that, yes, some of life's activities may seem meaningless (eg working hard all your life and never becoming rich), but what is important to God is not so much what you *do* as what you *are*. In fact, these inner attitudes are so important that straight after listing all of them to His disciples, Jesus tells them, in effect: *'You guys are awesome! Without you, the world will decay very quickly! Be the Beatitudes to a hurting world, and know what it means to truly live!'*

MON 2 JUN

37

PRAY

Lord Jesus, I realise that not everything in life is meaningless. My inner attitudes count for a great deal. I see now what things are important to You, so please help me to live out the Beatitudes in my relationships with others. Teach me to love people and the world as You do.

'... let God transform you into a new person by changing the way you think.'

KEY VERSE v2

TUES 3 JUN

38

THINK

Having your mind transformed by God is a process. It takes time because before we came to faith we each had many lies thrown at us by the world. So, don't be discouraged – it's not an overnight thing. The best we can pray in order to begin this process is to say, 'Father, transform my mind.'

Looking at yesterday's reading, we now know it's possible to live as 'salt and light' without losing our faith. The key is to focus on the big picture: what Jesus – not the world – says about us. If Jesus says we're truly happy by having the attitudes set out in the Beatitudes, then believe it!

Today we look at what Paul had to say to the first group of believers in Rome. The passage contains wise words, and hits on two things in particular. Firstly, if we're to survive in a crazy world, but also *live* in a way that honours God, we need to let Him transform the way we think. How? By reading truth (the Bible), talking to God (prayer) and hanging out with other believers (church). If we do this, we learn how to live godly lives; finding out how best we can serve God with the personalities and talents He's given us.

Secondly, Paul adds to this wisdom in verses 3–8 by explaining about humility. True humility means, instead of showing off, being honest about our strengths *and* weaknesses, and using our gifts and talents to love other people and live holier lives.

KEY VERSE v7

'Getting wisdom is the wisest thing you can do! And whatever else you do, develop good judgment.'

At the start of this week we explored a bit of Wisdom Literature as we looked at a passage from Ecclesiastes. Today we read some more, as we examine chapter 4 of the book of Proverbs.

You may have had moments in your life when you felt as though you were being pulled in all directions. You may feel like that now. You don't know which course of life to take, which college to go to or which career to head towards. Living is not easy! There are many conflicting voices in the world, each screaming for our attention.

Today's key verse is straight down the line. Set within a chapter exploring the benefits of wisdom, verse 7 speaks of it as something so precious that we should run after it with all we have. In the New Testament, the apostle James says if we need wisdom we should ask God (James 1:5).

So what is this wisdom? Well, it's the wisdom of knowing that we were created to live, serve and worship God. When we embrace this wisdom, we begin to go deeper in our relationship with God and learn to love and live among people of all backgrounds.

PRAY

Father, I want to have Your wisdom in my life, no matter what it costs! Help me to run after a relationship with You with all I've got. Help me to learn about how to truly live for You in this life and to love others and share this wisdom with them.

WED 4 JUN

39

'On the last day ... Jesus stood and shouted to the crowds, "Anyone who is thirsty may come to me!"'

KEY VERSE
v37

THURS 5 JUN

40

THINK

Imagine a drink that could quench your thirst forever without the need to drink again. This is the power of the Holy Spirit in us – a living water, a perfect wisdom, that teaches us how to live. Check out Isaiah 55:1–2 and see how Jesus fulfilled Isaiah's words.

At the end of the Festival of Shelters (a key celebration in the Jewish calendar) Jesus gets up and shouts to the crowd: 'Anyone who is thirsty may come to me!' What was He up to? Why did He start shouting like this during a busy, bustling festival?

In the days leading up to this, Jesus had been teaching in the Jewish Temple, but there were mixed feelings among the people there about His claims. Some said He was a good man, and that after all the miracles He had performed He might actually be the Messiah. Others said He couldn't be the Messiah as they knew where He was from. The true Messiah would be a man of mystery who would simply appear on the scene – He wouldn't be a carpenter's son.

Jesus knew the people's doubts, yet on the last day of the festival, He shouted out about the free gift of living water He would give to anyone who would believe in Him. In Ecclesiastes and Proverbs God shows us our need for wisdom, and in Matthew He shows us the cost of such wisdom. Here Jesus reveals the power He gives to help us live for Him; *true wisdom* comes from *living water*.

'... your former friends are surprised when you no longer plunge into the flood of wild and destructive things they do.'

Have you come in for any criticism because of your faith in Jesus? Maybe you've been exploring Christianity and your mates have made fun of you for this. Maybe you've suffered physical abuse for following Jesus.

Jesus never said that living for Him would be a bed of roses. He did, however, promise that He would never leave us during our lives on earth. In fact, right the way through the history of God's people, God has constantly reminded them of His love and faithfulness. (Check out Deuteronomy 31:6 and also Psalm 118:6.)

Peter writes to the believers throughout Asia in the first of his two encouraging letters explaining our future destiny as people of God. However, in verse 1, he doesn't mince his words. Jesus suffered, and because of this, we as His followers may do so too. We should be ready for a life that isn't easy living. In all circumstances, as people who now belong to God, we should live lives that are pleasing to God and serve others.

FRI 6 JUN

41

CHALLENGE

Read verses 7–9 again. How disciplined are you at the moment about praying? In what ways are you choosing to love rather than hold grudges against people? And what about hospitality – are you open and inclusive with people, offering to share what you have with them?

KEY VERSE
v10

'The thief's purpose is to steal and kill and destroy. My purpose is to give them a rich and satisfying life.'

Last week we explored living as salt and light, the importance of getting wisdom – no matter what it costs us – and also the free invitation of Jesus to receive living water. These things – salt and light, wisdom and living water – are all symbols which represent our developing a *living* relationship with the *living* God.

'Doing life' with God is the most amazing adventure we could ever have, yet even as Christians we can sometimes forget what fun this can be. When speaking to His followers, Jesus used many different ideas to illustrate deep truths. A lot of His followers were either fishermen or farmers, so He always used imagery that they could identify with quickly and easily.

In today's passage, Jesus describes Himself as the Good Shepherd. He says that the robber (Satan) tries to deceive the sheep (us believers) into following his voice instead of the Good Shepherd's.

Jesus was saying that Satan speaks through many things in the world today, telling us to follow him rather than God. So how do we hear God's voice among all the others screaming at us? Well, over the next week, we'll explore life within the church, life with Christian friends, and spending time alone with God – all vital ways we can strengthen our ability to hear Jesus' voice.

PRAY

Father God, I want to learn how to hear Jesus' voice. I realise that He came so that we could have a rich and satisfying life in relationship with You. Help me, through church, Christian friends and private time with You, to start living this life You freely offer me.

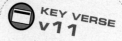

READING: Ecclesiastes 2:1–9

'But as I looked at everything ... it was all so meaningless ... There was nothing really worthwhile anywhere.'

KEY VERSE v11

Let's jump back to Ecclesiastes and spend a while examining some of the Teacher's claims. Today we read from chapter 2, where the Teacher (some scholars believe him to be King Solomon) talks about the worldly things he's pursued in search of happiness: laughter, wine, building projects, landscape gardening, farming, acquiring great wealth, and so on. It all seemed meaningless – empty, hollow and without spiritual worth.

So, who have we got here in this teacher? Does he suffer with depression or is he just a miserable person to hang out with? Is he ungrateful for all he's been privileged to enjoy in life or is there something more to him?

Here we have a man who loves God but isn't afraid to study the world around him and ask the deeper questions: *Why do people work all their life and achieve very little? Why do material goods fail to satisfy? Is there a time for war? Is there a time for peace? Why is life so unjust?*

As we explore the topic of 'Living', it's vital that in our own walk with God we develop an honesty with Him by asking the big questions.

CHALLENGE

As Christians, we need to keep eternity in mind. Our relationship with God means that when we die we will go to be with Him in heaven. Yet this promise shouldn't cause us to opt out of life now, but rather spur us on to live for God and lead others to Him.

**KEY VERSE
v10**

'Don't long for "the good old days."
This is not wise.'

Let's face it: life can be tough! We can look at
our lives now and feel overwhelmed by how
many things we've got to do or the problems
we have to overcome. We look to the future
and hope for happier, less stressful times
– maybe a holiday coming up or the end of
term – but the future is uncertain; anything
could happen. So what do so many of us do?
Simple. We look back to the 'good old days'.
We often remember the past as simple,
easy and full of fun – especially when we
select and focus on bits we enjoyed when our
present seems less enjoyable.

Today's passage lists a load of similar
nuggets of advice that seem at first a little
harsh, but on reflection are so wise. The
teacher is basically saying that life isn't
just about having a good time and going
to parties, although they are fun! We need
to remember that things may not always
be good, so at the end of the day it is only
wisdom – God's wisdom – that counts.

We all need to learn how to reflect on the
world around us. It is then that our own faith
in Jesus and His teachings can help make
sense of life's experiences.

TUES 10 JUN

45

THINK

Part of our living as Christians is to be earthy and real, not super-spiritual
and no earthly good to anyone. By reflecting on life and death, wealth and
poverty, war and peace and other vital issues, we begin to make sense of
the gift of life we've been given.

'Don't let the excitement of youth cause you to forget your Creator.'

KEY VERSE
v1

CHALLENGE

Do you know God now? Do you have a real relationship with Him today? You know, the best thing you can ever do is accept Jesus as your Saviour and give the rest of your life to Him. Don't risk growing old and missing out on a relationship with God who has so much to give you!

It's easy in life, especially when you're young, to forget about God. After all, when we're young we feel as though we can achieve anything – sometimes we even feel invincible. There's so much to see, so much to do and, when we look at how the years fly by, so little time in which to cram it all in. So, we naturally try and grab every opportunity that comes along.

The Teacher of Ecclesiastes makes some more 'opposite to the ways of the world' remarks. He tells us to remember God when we're young. Why? What's the point? There's too much to cram in already, isn't there? We can always turn to God just before we die and have a relationship with Him then, can't we?

Well, yes, we could wait until we're old to accept God, but it won't be as special as if we give our *whole* lifetime to Him. You see, what the Teacher is hinting at is that as humans get older, they get scarred. Life hurts. We fear crime, have emotional 'baggage' or maybe even physical ailments which can weigh us down, giving us a hard heart that's not open to God's love. We could die without knowing Him!

KEY VERSE v14

'God will judge us for everything we do, including every secret thing, whether good or bad.'

God's gift of life is amazing. We don't ask for it, and yet we're born into this world. We start as tiny babies and begin to make our way through life. Some of us take harder knocks than others, and some of us enjoy more privileges than others.

The Teacher's concluding remarks are the essence of why he has written the book of Ecclesiastes, showing us how we should view life. When we die, we will all have to stand and give a detailed account of how we have lived to the One who created us – God Almighty.

The Teacher devoted himself to *examining* and *experiencing* all that life has to offer. And compared to how amazing a relationship with God can be, he – as we now know – considers everything else meaningless. Wise advice, he describes, is painful yet helpful. Have you experienced this kind of advice? Perhaps a parent or friend has given you advice or said something that you really wish you hadn't heard but you know is true.

You always have the choice to accept wisdom or reject it. Verses 13 and 14 lay before us the final remarks of a very wise man!

THINK

What do you make of the Teacher? Do you agree with his remarks and take on life? What do you think about verses 13 and 14? How are you going to live the rest of your earthly life in the light of what they say?

'So you see, faith by itself isn't enough. Unless it produces good deeds, it is dead and useless.'

KEY VERSE
v17

FRI 13 JUN

48

As we conclude the first part of our study on 'Living', let's reflect on what we've learnt so far. We've looked at life through the eyes of the wise – our friend, the Teacher of Ecclesiastes. We've seen that without true friendship with God, life on earth can be pretty routine and often seem very harsh and 'meaningless'. We've also reflected on our faith, looking at what Jesus said about being 'salt and light', and examined Paul's comments on having our minds renewed by God.

In Part Two of 'Living', we're going to explore how we can get to grips with really living for God – actually getting stuck into doing what pleases Him on earth. One of the main things we'll look at is how we live out our faith practically. In today's reading, James writes to challenge his Jewish Christian friends in their faith. He says that it's not enough just to wish people well and to 'talk a good faith'. We need to prove God's love for people by what we actually *do* for them, for example, campaigning for social justice, ensuring the poor are fed and loved. More of this in Part Two!

PRAY

Father, thank You for all You've shown me about living so far. Help me put what I've learnt into practice by reflecting on my life and how I'm going to live the rest of it. Also, help me to see that living for You is not just about saying I believe in You, but giving You my everything.

KEY VERSE v7

'I have heard their cries of distress because of their harsh slave drivers. Yes, I am aware of their suffering.'

OBEYING

WEEKEND 14/15 JUN

49

Welcome to Part One of *Obeying*. Over two parts we'll look at how characters in the Bible learnt to obey God and how we too can do the same.

What drives a human being to obey, comply or conform to social patterns and behaviour? Social compliance is the act of obeying the law of the land as decided by authority. This might mean keeping to speed limits on roads, having a TV licence or fulfilling other legal requirements set by our government. When we conform to something, it may or may not be an actual written law. We may be conforming to an *expected* way of living that affects our behaviour – for example, giving up a seat on a

CONTINUED ▶

bus for a pregnant lady or elderly person.

As we look at the story of God's people and His laws, it is important to start at the very beginning. For 400 years the Hebrews were part of Eqyptian society, governed by their laws and conforming to their way of life. They are eventually forced into slave labour by a control-freak pharaoh. God hears their cries and puts into action the greatest escape plan of all time. The rest of Exodus fills in the details of this escape, but the result is that there are approximately 2 million Hebrews in the desert with no laws of society to live by, yet a loving God who now wants them to live in the best way – His way!

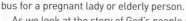

THINK

Would you call yourself an obedient person? Do you fight against rules and regulations (or social compliance) or are you cool with obeying them? What about God's way of life? Would you say that you're up for obeying everything He says about living life, or are there still things you don't quite agree with?

'He prayed three times a day, just as he had always done, giving thanks to his God.'

The world is quick to tell us what we *should* do, who we *should* be and how we *should* spend our money. We are constantly fed an advertising line of *Buy this shampoo and you will look great ... Wear this aftershave and you'll find love ...* However, despite all of this, none of us are forced to behave in a certain way. It is still just media pressure and not the law.

In today's passage, we see Daniel obeying God and praying three times a day. In doing this, he is disobeying the law of the land. Daniel's faith in God is in direct conflict with the will of King Darius.

In this country we have great freedom to meet together to worship, study the Bible, pray and even freely tell others about Jesus. In other countries of the world Christians do not have this type of freedom. Would you confess Jesus as Lord if your job were at stake? Would you stand up as a Christian if your family's life were at stake?

We all feel the media pressure to conform. However even under pressure and with his life at stake, Daniel obeyed God and disobeyed the law of the land.

MON 16 JUN

51

CHALLENGE

Daniel rightly puts his faith in God higher than his faith in King Darius. He is willing to die for obeying God. This is true obedience. In which areas of your life are you under pressure to conform rather than obeying God? Is your faith standing up – or is the pressure just too much?

'Let me ask you this one question: Did you receive the Holy Spirit by obeying the law of Moses?'

KEY VERSE
v2

TUES 17 JUN

52

What makes you a Christian? Church or youth group attendance? Reading your Bible and praying regularly? Simply being a good person?

All these things are important for Christians, but they do not *make* you a Christian. In the same way that going to McDonalds doesn't turn you into a hamburger, going to church won't transform you into a Christian.

Paul is trying to explain to the Christians in Galatia that we are saved through God's 'grace' not through obeying the law. We don't keep the 613 Jewish laws of the Torah in order to ensure that God loves us. We *know* God loves us because of Jesus' death on the cross and the gift of the Holy Spirit to us when we accepted Jesus into our lives.

We choose to obey God – not because we *have* to but because we *want* to! Our obedience is a clear indication of how much we love God and want to follow Him in every part of our lives. The Holy Spirit shows us how to live our lives in a way that pleases God and we obey God because of our great thankfulness and love for Him.

CHALLENGE

Do you obey God because you love Him? Unlike the Jews, we no longer have a set list of rules and regulations to follow. All we have to do is to love God with all our heart, soul, mind and strength and love our neighbour as ourselves (Mark 12:30–31). This is Jesus' teaching to us; commandments that should be a delight to obey!

KEY VERSE v7

'And as a sheep is silent before the shearers, he did not open his mouth.'

Why bother being obedient? Aren't laws and rules there to be broken? By obeying, can anything really happen? Isn't God being restrictive and unfair to us? Can we really obey a God who is so controlling?

The death of Jesus is the ultimate step of obedience: He is stripped of His clothes, beaten and whipped; a crown of thorns placed on His head, a robe on His blood-covered shoulders. Standing before Herod and Pilate He remained silent. Isaiah tells us that 'his life was cut short in midstream' (v.8) and that He did this to obey His Father's will – to bring all of humanity back into relationship with God.

At any point, Jesus could have called down legions of angels to rescue Him, but instead He obeyed the Father's plan. At any point, Jesus could have stepped off the cross and gone back into heaven, yet He obeyed. He could have halted time and space, yet He chose to obey His Father.

It is through Jesus' obedience that we are saved, rescued, forgiven and restored to the Father. Through His punishment we are set free.

WED 18 JUN

53

PRAY

Thank You, Lord Jesus, for Your death on the cross. Thank You that through Your obedience You took the punishment for me. Help me to be as obedient to You as You were to Your Father.

'For the Son of Man is Lord, even over the Sabbath!'

KEY VERSE
v8

THURS 19 JUN

54

PRAY

Father, help me not to be so concerned with obeying every single detail of the Christian life, that I fail to show grace, kindness and forgiveness to others. Help me to understand true obedience and the true freedom Your ways bring.

The disciples were hungry. They'd travelled with Jesus from place to place, away from their homes and family. They were hungry, young men (probably in their late teens, early twenties). According to the Pharisees, the act of taking the corn heads, rubbing them in their hands, blowing off the husks and eating the corn was equal to preparing a meal. Therefore they were guilty of 'breaking the Sabbath'.

The Pharisees were so wrapped up in a law-abiding lifestyle that they had lost sight of the One who had made the Law: God. Yet, even the mighty King David had broken this Law to allow his hungry troops to eat the bread from the house of God (v.3).

If the *letter* of the law is obeyed without the *essence* of the law being understood, then the *character* of the law-giver is not understood. Jesus answers the Pharisees, saying that He is the Lord of the Sabbath. It is He who gave Moses the laws to ensure that people could rest from domestic work, as well as be fed on the Sabbath. God is a kind law-giver, not a slave driver; yet the Pharisees failed to see this truth.

KEY VERSE v2

'I am the LORD your God, who rescued you from the land of Egypt, the place of your slavery.'

We are all known for a particular personality trait, skill, ability or quality. You may be really good at singing, fantastic at football, or abysmal at timekeeping. You may be known as someone's brother, sister, or child. Our identity is often noted by what we can do well, what we are good at or what we are not so good at.

Here we see the God of the Hebrews qualifying Himself before any laws or commandments are given: 'I am the LORD your God, who rescued you ...'

This perfect nine-word description sums up God in so many ways. It is God letting us know something of His personality.

The words 'I am' are so important when God describes Himself (Exod. 3:6) and later when Jesus describes Himself (John 8:12; 10:14; 14:6). He exists not just in the past (I was) but in the present and future.

He is also 'the LORD your God'. This term implies a relational, not a distant and uninterested, God. He is the God of the Hebrews and He is our kind, merciful, relational God today – a God we can obey with joy, who has our best interests at heart.

FRI 20 JUN

55

PRAY

Thank You, Lord, that You are a joy to obey – that You're not a God who commands obedience just for the sake of it. Rather, You ask us to obey because You have great things in store for our lives as we live them Your way.

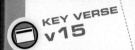

KEY VERSE v15

'But Jesus said, "It should be done, for we must carry out all that God requires." So John agreed to baptize him.'

Do you ever feel that there is an expectation on you as a person, maybe because of your parents or siblings, to adopt a certain behaviour or attitude? Do you struggle to have your own identity away from your family and friends? Do you feel a pressure to conform to a way of living that is just not you?

Try to imagine the expectation on Jesus to fulfil the prophecies that foretold His birth, His life, His death and His resurrection. In complete obedience, Jesus lays down His own will to 'carry out the will of the one who sent me' (John 5:30).

At the very beginning of His public ministry, Jesus

fulfils a prophecy about His being perfectly righteous. He had no need of baptism because He had not sinned. We are baptised to show that we have been brought over from death and sin into new life. Jesus had no sin – He was perfect! However, He went through the waters of baptism as a perfect example to us in all things (1 John 2:6; 1 Pet. 2:21) and suffered on earth to fulfil Isaiah's prophecy of the 'Suffering Servant' (Isa. 53).

Jesus' obedience is an example to us today. He lays aside His own will and follows the will of God His Father. He had the power to do anything, yet in everything He chose to obey God.

CHALLENGE

Does your will battle against the will of God? Is there a constant struggle within you to see who will win? Thank God today that you are not alone in this battle – that by the power of His Holy Spirit living in you, you can choose to obey Him.

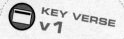

'Then Jesus was led by the Spirit into the wilderness to be tempted there by the devil.'

KEY VERSE
v1

MON 23 JUN

58

THINK

We worship a God who knows what temptation is. Jesus has felt temptation, yet in all cases He has chosen to obey God. (Read Hebrews 4:14–16.) God is not remote and distant, but understands how hard it is for us to obey.

Have you ever felt that God just doesn't understand – that He's remote from you and has no idea what you are actually going through? Well, these verses from Matthew 4 are for you.

In Genesis 3 we read the story of the temptation of Adam and Eve – by the serpent (the devil in disguise). In today's passage we see Jesus being tempted by the devil at the start of His public ministry. Jesus' obedience to God is being thoroughly tested by Satan.

The Bible tells us that after 40 days Jesus was hungry (v.2) and the devil came to Jesus to tempt Him in three ways. The first was the physical temptation of food at the end of a 40-day fast! Jesus was tempted to use His power to satisfy His physical hunger (v.3). The second temptation was spiritual; to throw Himself off the Temple and allow the angels to rescue Him (v.5) – in other words, to test the Father that He would truly look after Jesus' safety. The final temptation was obedience. Would Jesus kneel down and worship Satan in exchange for all the nations of the world (v.9)? Jesus' obedience was tested in every way possible and yet He still remained obedient.

KEY VERSE
v17

'I did not come to abolish the law of Moses or the writings of the prophets. No, I came to accomplish their purpose.'

I don't break laws, I bend them! How do you bend rules? Is it through telling what you call 'white lies'? Is it through copying others' homework? Is it through parking on yellow lines or the file sharing you've been doing recently?

God gave Moses a set of laws called the Ten Commandments. These laws helped the Hebrews to obey God and to love their fellow human beings. When Jesus appeared, it seemed that He came with a whole new set of rules and regulations but He was clear to point out that He was not a 'law breaker' but a 'law fulfiller'. He brought the Law to life by the way He taught us to live.

Through His teaching, He lived out the true meaning of the Law so that it impacted and challenged our lives. We may not be murderers, yet we've all experienced being angry with someone before (Matt. 5:21–22). We may not have committed adultery, but all of us have done things we're not proud of, or had thoughts that weren't pure (Matt. 5:27–28).

Jesus' teaching makes it clear that none of us are sinless; all of us are in need of the forgiving grace of Jesus through His victory on the cross.

TUES 24 JUN

59

CHALLENGE

Are you a law bender? Do you feel challenged about the way you do not obey God in everything? Confess to Him your sins and receive His forgiveness. We're not perfect, yet we can all receive forgiveness on a daily basis by coming to Jesus in prayer.

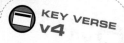

'You must not make for yourself an idol of any kind ...'

KEY VERSE v4

CHALLENGE

Draw out a 24-hour clock and estimate your time spent eating, studying, working, watching TV, playing computer games, spending time with friends and on the phone. Now look at how you spend your day. Is there much time for God?

The second commandment God gave the Hebrews was to do with idols. Remember that they'd lived in idol-infested Egyptian society for 400 years. The Egyptians worshipped their pharaoh as a living god and also worshipped a number of gods to encourage rain, to help them win wars or to help with fertility. All these gods, carved from wood and stone, constantly surrounded the Hebrews. The pressure for them to comply with the Egyptian method of worship was great.

The Hebrews had seen some amazing miracles performed by God: the many plagues sent on Pharaoh and his people, not to mention the parting of the Red Sea! Yet now, out in the wilderness, after all the drama had subsided, it would be easy for the Hebrews to do what the Egyptians did: set up an image of something to worship. However God strictly forbade them to do this because He, and no other, was their God.

If a hobby, ambition or relationship is taking over your time, money, thought life or Christian walk, then it is an idol. God says, 'You must not make for yourself an idol', but put Him first in your life.

'You must not misuse the name of the LORD your God. The LORD will not let you go unpunished if you misuse his name.'

It is impossible to sit through an episode of the American sitcom, *Friends*, without hearing the exclamation, 'Oh my God!' We are surrounded with blasphemous words, often spoken out of habit, but so easily becoming part of our everyday thought or speech life.

On the surface, this commandment doesn't look as important as murder, stealing and adultery. However, the Bible is clear that we shouldn't misuse God's name. The Jews were so full of reverent fear for God that they would use a different name for God (*Adonai* – meaning *My Lord*) rather than God's sacred name, *Yahweh*. They believed that the name of God was so important that any misuse of it was unforgivable!

With this in mind, how much do you treasure the wonderful name of Jesus?

Do you obey God, by honouring and standing up for His name? What about when your friends blaspheme in class – what will you say to them?

THURS 26 JUN

61

 CHALLENGE

If you are surrounded by peers who blaspheme, then why not challenge them to think about what they are saying. Tell them that it is offensive to you and to God. Use the situation to talk creatively about Jesus!

'Observe the Sabbath day by keeping it holy, as the LORD your God has commanded you.'

KEY VERSE
v 12

THINK

FRI 27 JUN

62

Can you organise your week so that you don't have to study on a Sunday? God created the universe in six days but on the seventh He continued to create – He created a day of rest. Do you create space for God on Sunday or another day in the week?

We live in a 24/7 society where it is possible to get anything at any time, day or night. We can shop on any day of the week; we have 24/7 entertainment on hundreds of TV channels, 365 days a year. Yet this was not in God's great plan for humankind. God's plan is to have a day set apart from the rest of our working week: a 'Sabbath' day when we spend time with God, rest up and reflect on life.

The reason we have the 'Sabbath' or, in our culture, a 'day of rest', is because of God's love and care for human beings. We are told in Genesis 2:2 that after the creation of the world God rested – so setting in place a system or routine to ensure a healthy work/life balance for the human race. He did this, not because He was tired, but because He knew our human limitations and our need for rest, as well as our desire to work.

God also blessed the Sabbath and made it holy. This means that Sunday, or any other day that we consider to be our Sabbath, is more than just a day to stay in bed late. It's one in which to remember God – to stop the busyness of life and spend time in His presence.

KEY VERSE
v36

'However, no one knows the day or hour when these things will happen ...'

END TIMES

We're returning to the subject of the *End Times* now and we'll focus on what Jesus had to *say* about this topic. With the more difficult aspects of Christianity, I always find it helpful to return to what Jesus said to His disciples because, more often than not, we find out what is really important and what is not worth our time bothering about!

CONTINUED ▶

Today's passage is just one of the key points that Jesus makes about the end of this present age, yet you'd be surprised how many people don't seem to take it seriously! On the news, from time to time, you may hear about those who claim that they've discovered the date for the end of the world. In fact, many people spent too much time believing that the turn of the year 2000 would see the end of time! However, Jesus categorically states that even He doesn't know when this current age will end and that only God the Father knows. So, rather than getting caught up analysing possible dates, Jesus removes this from our 'need to know list', encouraging us instead to be ready all the time.

After all, if we knew exactly when Jesus was coming back we'd be tempted to give up talking to others about Him, or we might make a sudden last-minute recommitment after spending most of our life abusing our minds and bodies.

THINK

It's good that we don't know when Jesus is coming back as it means that we remain motivated in our Christian life. So don't waste time on dates and times, but spend time getting ready for Jesus to return. Be brave and ask God to show you the areas of your life that might need some 'readying' for Jesus' return. Ask Him to help you deal with them through the power of His Holy Spirit.

KEY VERSE v21

'You won't be able to say, "Here it is!" or "It's over there!" For the Kingdom of God is already among you.'

In talking about the End Times, Matthew, Mark, Luke and John all use the phrase the *kingdom of God* or the *kingdom of heaven* to describe God's kingdom finally coming on earth. They also use it to record Jesus' description of the coming kingdom. Yet, if you read the passage and key verse, you might think that Luke has made an error, since they appear to contradict each other.

The main passage talks about the kingdom as still to come, but the key verse says that the kingdom of God is already here among us. This apparent mistake is actually an amazing piece of teaching! Rather than being either/or, the kingdom of God is in fact *both* here among us now and also *still to come!* A piece of the kingdom is now held within us, which we take with us everywhere, into every situation, as 'kingdom bearers', yet the fulfilment of God's kingdom on earth will be at the return of Christ. Christians use the phrase the 'now and the not yet' to describe this teaching.

When thinking about the coming kingdom, remember that through Jesus you have a part of that kingdom within you, which will be completed when He returns or you meet Him after death.

Lord, help me get my head around this double-sided kingdom.

MON 30 JUN

PRAY

KEY VERSE
v36

'Keep alert at all times.'

Have you ever been in a situation where you had to keep watch? Maybe it was playing Hide and Seek; or maybe you were simply waiting for someone, looking out for their arrival. It's amazing how the slightest noise or glimpse of movement focuses our attention, as our senses are heightened and we're more aware of what's going on around us.

Jesus encourages us to be this alert all the time, not only for His return but also for those lifestyle dangers we're often exposed to – such as drunkenness, constant partying or even worry. If we're tuned in to the warning signs that precede these things, then it's less likely we'll give in to temptation. Yet, if we remain blind to these dangers, it can be easy to end up somewhere we weren't expecting to be!

However, the bonus of being alert for Jesus' return and focusing on Him is that we can also experience the way in which our spiritual senses are heightened. Potential pitfalls in life seem more obvious, becoming easier to avoid. Furthermore, our problems start to seem a lot smaller!

TUES 1 JUL

66

CHALLENGE

Are there situations coming up this week that might be potential pitfalls for you? If so, pray about them and ask God to help you to stay alert and to overcome any temptation.

'For as the lightning flashes in the east and shines to the west, so it will be when the Son of Man comes.'

When I was younger, I became afraid, for a few months, that I'd miss the return of Jesus. Firstly, I was convinced that Jesus was coming back within my lifetime and, secondly, I was scared that He'd arrive in the middle of the night and I'd sleep right through it!

It sounds silly now, as I write this, since today's key verse shows us that not a single person will miss the coming of the Lord. As in a massive lightning storm, the entire sky from east to west will be lit up with the return of Jesus. This also helps us to handle situations in the future whereby someone might claim to be Jesus. Clearly, no one else would ever be able to return in that fashion! Jesus Himself told us what to expect, therefore people claiming falsely to be the Messiah aren't even worth a second glance.

We can be sure that there will be people who claim to be the Messiah, yet Jesus says that when the one and only Messiah does return, no one will need to double-check because everyone will know! We're not going to miss this heavenly light show if we're still on earth when Jesus returns!

WED 2 JUL

67

PRAY

Lord God, thank You for Your Son. I pray that my non-Christian friends might also realise that Jesus is their Saviour and Lord. Help me to communicate this to them; to take courage and demonstrate You through the way I live my life.

'But all this is only the first of the birth pains, with more to come.'

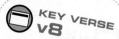

KEY VERSE
v8

CHALLENGE

Read, watch or browse some news channels. Pray about the situations you see before you and thank God that, despite the horror, He is still in control of world events.

We've already seen that Jesus Himself said that He didn't know exactly when the Father would send Him back to earth. However, He did provide us with some signs to look out for that will help us to understand that the time of His return is drawing near.

In today's passage there are three signs that Jesus provides to help us. The first is one we touched on yesterday – deceivers. Many will falsely claim to be Jesus. The second is that there will be wars and rumours of wars, events that we can agree are occurring all around the world today. The third sign is that there will be famines and earthquakes all over the world. This, again, is something that we see currently happening in places like the Sudan, Ethiopia and Bangladesh.

These events bring a tremendous amount of suffering and struggle for many across the globe, but we are told by Jesus not to panic, as these signs are merely the beginning of the end. Just as the first contraction lets a woman know that she's about to give birth, these signs let the world know that Jesus is preparing to return.

'Sin will be rampant everywhere, and the love of many will grow cold.'

In today's passage, there are three further signs provided by Jesus that indicate the time of His return. These three signs are directed towards the Church, whereas the previous three were focused on the world at large.

Firstly, Christians will be persecuted, arrested and killed for their faith. It's hard to know what living as a hated minority would be like. Our Western world was founded on Christian morality, yet in much of the rest of the world, Christians have constantly struggled against persecution from the state.

Secondly, many Christians will turn away from the faith. It's going to become harder to be a Christian. For some, it will be too hard and they'll give up.

Thirdly, people within the Church will deceive many with false teaching and wrong thinking. Christians are going to have to constantly come back to the truth of the Bible.

Whilst we should be aware of these things, don't be scared! But rather, stay close to God and be encouraged to keep going until the end when you will at last be with Jesus.

FRI 4 JUL

69

CHALLENGE

Encourage a fellow Christian – write an email to a missionary from your church or simply send a text to a friend. It's hard to live out your faith in today's climate – let someone know that you are thinking of them. We all need encouragement.

KEY VERSE v10

'For the Good News must first be preached to all nations.'

Telling the world about Jesus can seem like an impossible task sometimes. There are so many nations and people groups that it can all get a little overwhelming. Yet Jesus makes it clear in today's passage that the good news about His kingdom *will* be preached throughout the world and that's a promise He will fulfil. He never goes back on His word!

It does mean, though, that we all have some work to do! I have a friend who is a missionary in Kenya, where she works with children who have been disabled from birth or by an accident. She's always wanted to go to Africa and be a missionary, to tell others about the love that Jesus has for them. I admire her courage

and strength. She, like many others, takes the good news about Jesus to other nations. However, we don't all need to go abroad to be missionaries to tell others about our Saviour. Each day, in small ways, we can be missionaries by communicating to our friends and family the truth we have experienced in our own lives.

People cannot argue with your own experience of Jesus being your Saviour. They might not like it, but it's *your* truth. It's something they have to accept – and maybe even want for themselves. We just have to be confident in our faith and in what we have experienced of Jesus – being ready to tell others when the opportunities arise.

PRAY

Ask God to give you an opportunity to talk to a friend about the way in which Jesus has impacted your life.

'To those that use well what they are given, even more will be given ...'

KEY VERSE
v29

THINK

What talents or abilities do you have that you would like to use in building the kingdom of God? If you are unsure of your abilities, ask God to show you. Be confident that God knows the gifts you have. He will use you, if you surrender these gifts for His service.

In continuing to talk about the End Times, Jesus not only points out that we'll be the ones preaching the good news of the kingdom (as we saw yesterday) but also talks to us about the attitude in which we should build His kingdom.

Today's passage about the parable of the three servants provides a practical picture of how we should handle what God has entrusted to us in the way of finance, gifts, ability or talent. Some of us have astounding talent – enough to make us the next 'Pop Idol' (5 bags of silver). Others have expert skill with figures and may become successful accountants (2 bags); whilst still others are not so gifted (1 bag), yet are still able to be of use to God.

We can all help to build the kingdom on earth and get back double what we put in! What we must not do is to hide away, becoming afraid of what might happen when Jesus returns. It's better to put our all into building the kingdom and to go against what the world sees as success, rather than to live a safe, but boring, life where we bury our abilities instead of using them for God's glory.

KEY VERSE
v34

'Then the King will say to those on his right, "Come, you who are blessed by my Father, inherit the Kingdom ..."'

Today we see Jesus describing that final day when He returns in glory to judge the world, separating those who have loved and served Him from those who have rejected Him. It is a powerful picture of how our responsibilities to those around us in this life impact upon our future in God's eternal kingdom. How we treat the poor, the hungry, the sick, the imprisoned and the thirsty is important to Jesus. Loving Jesus compels us to love others, no matter what they are like, because we know that Jesus first loved us, despite all the sin and muck in our lives.

When we reach out to those the rest of society rejects, we show the love of Jesus. That's why Jesus says, '... when you did it to one of the least of these ... you were doing it to me!' (v.40)

Poverty might never be history until Jesus comes again, but we all can contribute to helping people who are sick, hungry, thirsty or in prison. Our eternal inheritance in God's kingdom seems to be directly related to how far we go to help others here on earth. Although eternal life is a gift of God's grace, our faith should be shown in love for others.

THINK

Who could you help? Maybe you could volunteer for a charity, or donate to a project overseas – the opportunities are endless!

'People will be terrified at what they see coming upon the earth ...'

KEY VERSE
v26

WED 9 JUL

74

PRAY

Thank and praise God that He created the world and knows everything about it – including you!

Have you ever watched an episode of a supernatural drama or a spooky film? They contain eerie moments when certain dramatic elements signal that someone is going to die or something is about to occur. The music slows down, the characters hold their breath, waiting, then ... bang! Whatever it is that was about to happen suddenly happens – and we still jump off our seats!

In many ways, today's passage, written again in pictorial, symbolic language, demonstrates how the whole of creation will be affected by the second coming of Jesus. Scholars disagree as to how literally to take these descriptions. Signs and wonders may include roaring seas, strange tides and weird goings on with the sun, moon and stars. Earth may seem like part of a scary movie whilst awaiting the return of its Creator. Jesus tells us that people will be terrified by what happens. Yet, as Christians, we can be assured that God is still in control and can trust that He will be with us, whatever happens. 'Don't be afraid for I am with you ... I will strengthen you and help you' (Isa. 41:10).

The only person that can usher in our new earth is Jesus – so we need not fear anything else!

'But you will receive power when the Holy Spirit comes upon you.'

We're venturing outside the Gospels of Matthew, Mark and Luke today to pay a quick visit to the book of Acts, where we see Jesus talking to His disciples just before He returns to heaven. Jesus repeats His instruction not to worry about dates and times, before He mentions that they will receive power from the Holy Spirit to continue the work of spreading the news about the kingdom of God.

The disciples, on seeing Jesus after His resurrection, were checking to see whether this was the return that Jesus had spoken about in Matthew 24. However, Jesus says 'not yet' – and tells them about their new role as witnesses about Him to the whole world, encouraging them that they will not be alone.

There is a trap that we fall into as Christians. We easily forget that we have company in our mission to tell the world about Jesus. The Holy Spirit comes to us, as a gift from the Lord. He comes to give us great power and passion in all that we do as we live for the Father's glory. So in thinking about the End Times and the instructions that Jesus gave about them, we should always be asking the Holy Spirit to grant us power to tell others about Him.

THURS 10 JUL

75

PRAY

Holy Spirit, please give me the power I need to reach out to my friends and tell them about Jesus.

'And they will see the Son of Man coming on the clouds of heaven with power and great glory.'

KEY VERSE
v30

FRI 11 JUL

THINK

Skim through these notes again and pull out the bits that encouraged you the most in your faith.

Over the past couple of weeks we've looked in detail at what Jesus told us about the End Times. We've seen that He has given us signs to be aware of, descriptions of what the End Times may look like and what He asks of us in the meantime.

There's been a lot to think about and I hope that you've discovered things you hadn't seen before. When it comes to understanding the End Times, there's plenty to grasp and we've only really touched on a few aspects of this subject.

In today's passage Matthew shares an image of Jesus returning on the clouds in great glory and gathering all His followers to Himself. There are days when I would love Jesus to come back now and there are others when I'm happy if He leaves it a few more years. Yet nothing quite beats the idea of the Lord Jesus, who loves you and me, coming back to gather us – His chosen ones – together to be with Him. He loves you and wants to see you face to face. Come, Lord Jesus!

KEY VERSE v7

'I will give it all to you if you will worship me.'

LEADING

Welcome back to Part Two of *Leading*. Are you ready to take a further look at what makes a good leader and how we can grow in the ability to lead others in the faith?

Influence is at the core of leadership. However, historical figures like Hitler, Mao and Kim Jong II carried great influence but did not use it as a force for good. Influence needs to be balanced by character. Good character can often be measured by patience and humility, which is why the Scriptures show us that people in positions of leadership need to be clothed in such qualities. Even Jesus was tested by Satan: would He worship Satan in return for glory and authority over the kingdoms of the world? Jesus leads us by His example. His godly character could not be swayed by temptation.

CONTINUED ▸

Let's think now about the life of Joseph (Gen. 37; 39–50). We may already know a little of his amazing story, with its many ups and downs, twists and turns. Eventually, by the time he is 30, he stands in Pharaoh's presence and is made ruler of Egypt, second only to Pharaoh himself.

Joseph served his time as a slave, a ruler of a government official's household, then as a wrongly-accused prisoner, and finally even as Prime Minister of Egypt! His character was refined, through difficult circumstances, and he was made wiser. Eventually, using his influence as a leader, he rescued the nation of Israel, including his own father and brothers, from serious famine. What a leader!

THINK

There's an old story of a Chinese lady explaining to her daughter that Christians can be like a carrot, an egg or a tea bag. In the hot water of difficult circumstances our toughness can soften like a carrot or our heart can become hardened like an egg. Or thirdly; like a tea bag, we can change the flavour of the hot water around us. Do circumstances get you down or do you allow them to build strength into your character?

'No one needed to tell him what mankind is really like.'

What's the next characteristic in a good leader after influence and character? Knowing people! Do you know people? Not just individuals or groups of people, but what people, in general, are like? Do you understand people: what makes them tick, how to listen to them, how to communicate with them?

Jesus knew people. He understood human nature and, as a result, He knew how to engage with people. In the Gospels, Jesus is asked hundreds of questions and He appears to only reply directly to a handful. The rest of the time He communicates with people in a way that cuts through their pretence – answering back with questions that go directly to the heart of the matter.

Listening doesn't mean being swayed by what is being said. It means that you value the person speaking. Good leaders engage well with other people. Listening and knowing what someone is saying is more than just hearing. A large proportion of what is being said is communicated in nonverbal ways, through body language, tone of voice and choice of words. Good leaders listen between the lines and take time to measure their response.

MON 14 JUL

79

CHALLENGE

Do you listen to people? Listening is a key aspect of communication. Check your body language when someone is telling you something. Are you focused on what they are saying? Do you make eye contact? Are you distracted or focusing on something else?

'You are seeing things merely from a human point of view, not from God's.'

KEY VERSE
v23

PRAY

Lord, I pray for Christians around the world who suffer for their faith. Help me to have the same faith and to be faithful to the calling You have given me – whether it be sharing Jesus with my mates, befriending a person with no friends or suffering for what I believe in.

Jesus had just been outlining to His disciples the bigger picture; the Father's plan for Jesus' mission on earth. Up until now, the story had been all good. People were being healed. There was radical new preaching and multitudes of fans following them all across the countryside. Now Jesus starts to talk about suffering, death and resurrection. The disciples, led by Peter, try to dissuade Jesus from going through with the plan.

After saying yes to Jesus and choosing the Christian faith, you need to persevere and endure. Peer group pressure is a powerful thing. The disciples tried to influence Jesus. Having made your decision to live in a certain way or do a certain thing, keep in mind the bigger picture and don't be turned aside by anything or anyone.

Around 200 million Christians live in countries where, at any time, they could face persecution for their faith. Yet, for the bigger vision of following Christ, they will not be dissuaded by argument, propaganda, exclusion from their family, physical beatings or even death. They lead through their strong faith.

KEY VERSE v1

'Who may worship in your sanctuary, LORD? Who may enter your presence on your holy hill?'

We've explored *Influence*, *Character* and *People*. Now let's look at *Persistence* as a leadership quality. In management speak, persistence gets called 'drive', yet it's all about keeping on until a job gets done. Alternative words would be commitment, endurance and perseverance – holding to your promise even when it hurts, as the psalmist says.

Miguel Kashlan was the only evangelist in a place called San Juan Chamula in Southern Mexico. Fierce persecution broke out against his new Christian church, yet Miguel continued to share the gospel with everyone.

As persecution increased, he bought land in a safe area to house all the Christian refugees. He was becoming a nuisance to his enemies. They wanted him dead. He was kidnapped as he went about his shopping. As he was taken he shouted to nearby Christians, 'They have taken me, but do not fear. Carry on and I will see you again.' Miguel Kashlan was then taken to the hill country and killed for preaching the gospel.

CHALLENGE

This is an extreme example of persistence and endurance. It is said, 'If you have nothing you are willing to die for, then you have nothing to live for.' What are your convictions? What do you believe is true and worth living for 100% – or even dying for?

'Look, I am sending you out as sheep among wolves. So be as shrewd as snakes and harmless as doves.'

KEY VERSE v16

After persistence, what else could you need to be a leader? Well, wisdom is a great quality for any leader to have! In this reading, Jesus is preparing and sending out His disciples, basically saying: 'Look guys, you're going out into dangerous territory now. Be smart about what you're doing!' Jesus was not saying 'Be really cautious, hesitant and scared' but 'Have your wits about you. Be streetwise!'

The Bible was not printed in English until the early sixteenth century, when William Tyndale risked his life to provide the common person with the Bible. The Church hunted him down, believing that God's Word should only be read in Latin or Greek. Tyndale fled England and went to the continent where he continued translating and printing copies of the English Bible, which were later smuggled back into England.

The Church bought all the copies at inflated prices on the black market and burnt them. However, Tyndale sneakily used this money to improve his translation and produce even more Bibles that later flooded the country!

THURS 17 JUL

82

THINK

Winkie Pratney, author and youth speaker, once said, 'Becoming a Christian is about RENEWING your mind not REMOVING your mind.' Being practically wise is something Jesus tells us to be. Do we try and distance ourselves from streetwise people or can we learn a thing or two from them?

KEY VERSE v4

'I am writing to Titus, my true son in the faith that we share.'

How do you develop as a leader? There are a few options available; one or all of which may be helpful to you.

The first is to do some classroom leadership training – have a teacher tell you about being a leader. This is great, but chances are that the teacher is perhaps not a great leader; they might only know the academic stuff they studied at teacher training college.

You could try being thrown in at the deep end – the *sink or swim* method – and convince someone to 'throw' you into a leadership situation. That's to say, convince someone to give you an opportunity for leadership with some responsibility, then see if you can survive and stay afloat.

Or you could take a look around you: look at who inspires you, who you would follow as a leader and learn directly from them. Notice how they do things and the people skills they have. Ask them questions and mull over the answers.

Go for it! Like Titus learnt from Paul, find godly examples of leadership and make it your goal to learn to be a leader using one or all of the above options.

FRI 18 JUL

83

PRAY

Lord, I want to be a leader. Help me to learn to be the kind of leader You would have me to be. Please give me leaders to learn from and situations in which to develop leadership character.

KEY VERSE v6

'David was now in great danger ... they began to talk of stoning him. But David found strength in the LORD his God.'

A major part of developing leadership is developing the ability to lead yourself – otherwise known as self-control. This is what kicks in when life's challenges come along.

David and his men return to find their homes raided and their wives and children taken. On top of that, David's men blame him and start to turn on him. However, David strengthens himself in God. Ever noticed how many times Jesus' busy schedule was punctuated with times of withdrawal and prayer?

Wang Mingdao, a famous Chinese evangelist

– imprisoned for 20 years for being a Christian during the Cultural Revolution – offers this advice: 'Build yourself a cell.' What does he mean? Most of his imprisonment was solitary confinement, for periods long enough to break people's faith, yet he remained strong. On his time in prison he said, 'Everything that had given me meaning as a Christian worker had been taken away from me. And I had nothing to do. Nothing to do except get to know God. And for 20 years that was the greatest relationship I have ever known. But the cell was the means.'

CHALLENGE

Wang Mingdao talked of a cell as a means to be clear of distractions in order to focus fully on God, just like Jesus did. What priority do you put on spending time with God? Is it top priority? Does your organisation of time reflect this? Where do you go to meet with God?

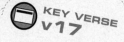

'Obey your spiritual leaders, and do what they say. Their work is to watch over your souls ...'

KEY VERSE v17

PRAY

Father, there are a lot of people in authority over me. I pray for them that their job will be made easier by how I respond to their leading. Help me to become a better leader by learning to respect authority myself.

How many people actually have some sort of authority over you? Think about it. Parents? Teachers? Youth group leaders? How about the police? Who else? Maybe a supervisor at work? That's a few to be thinking about for now!

For the most part, people in authority over us are there for our benefit. Parents are our guardians. They raise us. Teachers are simply there to educate us. This is a good thing no matter how we may feel about attending school or college. Then there is the informal kind of authority – like, for instance, if you go to a youth group and are guided by leaders. They are there for your benefit. Finally, the police are there for your benefit and the benefit of society.

Yet, something inside of us always seems to kick against authority. *'Why are they trying to tell me what to do?'* Authority can be so frustrating, but actually it is to our benefit that we at least try and make their job of leading easier. The easier they find their job the better we will be led.

KEY VERSE v23

'But the mob shouted louder and louder, demanding that Jesus be crucified, and their voices prevailed.'

Pontius Pilate: history remembers him in an unfavourable light. He buckled under pressure from the crowd and officially sent Jesus to a brutal death. He could find no reason for Jesus to die and yet he let the crowd have its way.

Pressure has an amazing capacity to make us sell ourselves short of what we believe. Peer pressure makes us go along with the crowd and take the path of least resistance.

It is difficult, but when it comes to our faith, we cannot sell ourselves short to follow the crowd. If we firmly believe something, then to compromise is a bit like denying who we actually are and the God we follow. You might befriend a kid at school, who no one else likes, because you have compassion. However, if you give in later to the ridicule and ignore this kid in front of your mates, it would mean that you'd buckled under pressure.

If you want to be a leader, you have to be willing to leave the crowd and make your own choices based on your own convictions. This will also help you to develop your identity as a person in your own right.

TUES 22 JUL

87

CHALLENGE

Do you bow to peer pressure all the time? Does it leave you feeling hollow, maybe even guilty? It's not always necessary to go against the grain and be singled out, but sometimes you have to make a stand for your beliefs no matter what the cost. Are you willing to do this?

'And then, though it is against the law, I will go in to see the king. If I must die, I must die.'

KEY VERSE v16

Esther became a queen because of her beauty, but she became a leader – in the truest sense – because of her courage. Her resolve to do what was right, even though it might have cost her her life, was inspirational.

What situation are you in right now? Do you need courage to make it through? Do need something to help steady your resolve to do what is right? Are people you know at risk from something? Do you have the power to provide a solution?

Sometimes, in order to rise up and lead, we need encouragement. When he took over from Moses as 'CEO of Exodus Ltd', Joshua needed all the encouragement he could get. He was now responsible for leading an entire nation of grouchy people, surrounded by enemies and wandering around in the middle of nowhere, to the promised land. What does God say to encourage him? 'This is my command – be strong and courageous! Do not be afraid or discouraged. For the LORD your God is with you wherever you go' (Josh. 1:9).

Are you willing to use every leadership skill you possess to help others?

PRAY

Lord, give me courage and help me to know that You are with me wherever I may go. Help me to be courageous in order to lead people, and not to think about what I might lose by helping others.

KEY VERSE v32

'"Don't worry about this Philistine," David told Saul. "I'll go fight him!"'

Leadership is not about being at the top or being called leader. It is not a name or a position to enjoy. For days the Israelite army have been sitting on their heels, demoralised by a giant Philistine constantly yelling abuse at them and their God. Saul is the king (and a huge warrior himself at that!) and he has not led them anywhere. He's scared. They're all scared! Goliath is huge!

David, just a kid, pops up and says: 'No worries, I'll handle this.' He rolls up his sleeves, gets out his sling and the rest, as we say, is history.

From the moment David kills Goliath, the army of Israel take courage, draw new strength from what they've just seen and go on to rout the Philistines. So, who was the real leader here – King Saul or the 'Shepherd Boy', David?

You too can make a difference, no matter what age you are, position or title you have or don't have. This could be by practical acts of kindness to those who need help, or it could be by standing up and volunteering to lead in a situation. Seize the situation and simply lead by example!

Where can you make a difference today? When you've thought about it, take courage and lead!

THURS 24 JUL

89

THINK

'Be an example to all believers in what you say, in the way you live, in your love, your faith, and your purity.'

KEY VERSE
v12

FRI 25 JUL

PRAY

Father, thank You for who I am. Allow me to see that I am important to all You plan for this world and for those around me. Help me to *lead* in my life, seeking Your wisdom and giving You the glory. Amen.

As we come to the end of our look at leading, what have we learned?

Leadership is about identity and character. Firstly we need to be secure in God's love and in how much He values us just for who we are.

Leadership is about doing. It is not just a title, but wise action that others can follow.

Leadership is about example. It may not always be 'up front', in a recognised way, but can be how we act with our family, friends and strangers, at work, college, uni etc.

Leadership is about influence. Being looked up to, copied and 'followed' in daily life by younger siblings and, later on in life, by our children. How do you use your authority over others?

Leadership is about vision. Seeing the big picture and being willing to communicate what we see so that it can be achieved – no matter what setbacks are encountered.

Leadership is about serving. Having the courage to serve others whilst following the example Jesus set.

Leadership is about you. Whether you think of yourself as a born 'leader' or not, whether you are an introvert or extrovert, you will lead in some aspect of your life. Be sure to make a difference.

KEY VERSE
v14

'Instead, clothe yourself with the presence of the Lord Jesus Christ.'

LIVING

Welcome back to the second part of *Living*. Over the next fortnight we're going to be examining what it means to live all out for Jesus, studying some passages from Paul's letter to the believers in Rome, Thessalonica, Colosse, Ephesus and Philippi. So, let's get going and let's get living!

In today's reading, we get a snippet of Paul's letter to the church in Rome. Paul was a Roman citizen by birth, and he passionately loved the believers in that city, wanting them to be the very best they could be for God. In chapter 13, Paul is addressing two main issues: respect for authority and the requirement God places on us simply to love people.

CONTINUED ▸▸

When it comes to living all out for Jesus, this passage couldn't put things any clearer. In verse 12 Paul says that our salvation is nearer now than it ever was (whether this means your own death and going to be with Jesus, or His return to earth), and that it's now time to get rid of our ungodly lifestyles and exchange them for 'the shining armour of right living'. Why armour? Well, Paul recognises that it's not easy to live out your faith in this ungodly world, yet when we *choose* to live for God, He gives us the strength (the armour) to resist the world, through the very act of obeying Him.

CHALLENGE

At the start of this second part of *Living*, are you up for the challenge of examining your own life and how you're currently living it? Are you prepared to compare it to what the Bible says about right living? This exercise is not designed to make you feel bad or condemned, but to encourage healthy comparison, because we know that with God's help we can make important changes to our lifestyle.

KEY VERSE
v7

'For we don't live for ourselves or die for ourselves.'

Today's key verse sounds a bit odd doesn't it? Let's set it in its proper context. We know from yesterday that in chapter 13 Paul talked about the importance of respecting authority and living to love others. In chapter 14, Paul switches to talk about how we should avoid criticising others and judging some of the things they believe to be OK or not OK for them to do as Christians.

Paul is passionate about telling us that not every issue is crystal clear in the Christian faith. Some Christians will do things we think are wrong, others may have a problem with what *we* do. The key point Paul is making is that we should conduct ourselves wisely around Christians who don't always do things our way, and we should avoid judging them for how they live. Instead – and now we get to verse 7 – we should appreciate that in this life we don't live or die for ourselves, rather we aim to become the very *best* we can be for God. We need to live for Him with everything we've got, and that means respecting how other believers live out their faith.

MON 28 JUL

93

THINK

People express Christianity differently. Obviously there are things that are definitely wrong (stealing, lying, sexual sin, and so on), yet there are areas that the Bible is not clear on. We need to respect the different ways people live for Jesus.

'Make it your goal to live a quiet life, minding your own business ...'

KEY VERSE v11

TUES 29 JUL

94

Jumping across from Paul's letter in Romans to his first letter to the Thessalonians, we find some very practical advice on how to live. In our passage for today, Paul outlines for his friends his teaching on living to please God.

We live in an age where it's all about 'me'; how can I best please *myself*? What's in it for *me*? How do *I* look? Who fancies *me*? What did they say about *me*? Paul tells his friends in Thessalonica to live in a way that pleases God (v.1), to be holy (v.3), to control their bodies (vv.4–5) and to not cheat people (v.6). In verses 7–8, Paul again states that God has called us believers to live holy lives, and anyone who doesn't is not disobeying human teaching but actually disobeying God!

In verses 9–10, Paul, like any amazing friend, encourages the Thessalonians. He tells them that God has taught them to love each other, and they are great at it! *'Keep it up,'* he urges.

Finally, in a lesson to us all, he encourages us to live quiet lives that simply get on with living and loving for God, so that non-Christians will respect the way we do things.

PRAY

Father, it's hard to live to please You when I can so easily be caught up in my own world. Please help me to quietly get on with living to please You, and to be busy only in loving and serving others.

KEY VERSE
v18

'Be thankful in all circumstances, for this is God's will for you who belong to Christ Jesus.'

Yesterday we looked at part of Paul's first letter to the believers in Thessalonica. Today we'll take another glimpse at this letter, looking at Paul's closing remarks to his friends. These are simple instructions on living out a godly life.

At the end of the previous chapter, Paul spoke about the resurrection, and starts the chapter we're looking at today by looking at Christ's return. As a closing piece he gives his friends some advice that is also meant for us believers today. In verse 12, we're told to honour our Christian leaders who guide and serve us. We're told to respect them. Do you respect your church leaders? We're told to live peacefully with each other. Are you living peacefully with your brothers and sisters in Christ, or do you need to say sorry for things that have come between you?

Finally, we're told to encourage the shy, to be patient, not to take revenge on people, to always be joyful and to never stop praying. We're to be thankful in all circumstances, allow the Holy Spirit to work through us and stay away from every kind of evil.

WED 30 JUL

95

CHALLENGE

Read through the passage again. Imagine you're in the congregation at Thessalonica and have just received Paul's letter to read. How do you feel about living now? It's quite a challenge, isn't it? What can you do to better serve God and others?

'Keep a close watch on how you live and on your teaching.'

KEY VERSE v16

THURS 31 JUL

96

Paul had a protégé called Timothy. Paul was his mentor in becoming a church leader. Timothy was a young guy with the gift of leadership and Paul, who'd had experience in this area, wanted to ensure that Timothy kept to the right path of living for God while coping with the pressures of leading others.

Now, not every one of us is a leader. We won't all pastor church congregations. Yet there are lessons for all of us to learn from Paul's care for Timothy. We are all on the road of faith, and at some point – maybe even now – we will have responsibility for mentoring others. Are you helping to lead a cell group, Youth Alpha, Art Of Connecting or a Christian Union? Do you have a non-Christian mate who bombards you with questions about life after death?

We'll all find ourselves in situations where we need to mentor others. Just because you're young, don't think you've no wisdom to pass on! Above all, though, as it says in verse 16, we must keep a close eye on our own walk with Jesus so that we can be the best for those who we will help in their faith.

PRAY

Father, I realise I'm no expert in Christian living, yet I know You want me to be at my best so I can help others in their faith. Help me to keep an eye on what I believe, to learn more about You from study and prayer and to be wise in the example I set to others of Christian living.

KEY VERSE
v17

'With the Lord's authority I say this: Live no longer as the Gentiles do, for they are hopelessly confused.'

Switch on the TV for five minutes and you'll hear the latest celebrity gossip. What or who are these people really living for? Do they have a purpose or a philosophy for life, or do they simply wander from one expensive shopping trip to the next?

Paul wrote to the believers in Ephesus (a bustling, multicultural trading city at the gateway of Europe and Asia) with some counter-cultural teaching for being a Christian in a very godless environment. He outlines in verses 17–19 the way confused, non-Christian people live, but goes on to say, 'Listen guys, you're not like them! That's not what you've learnt. So if you've been slipping back into old ways of living, get rid of the old nature and put on the new!'

Paul then gets very practical: 'If you're a thief, quit stealing stuff. If you've got a problem with bad language, learn to use language to encourage people instead.'

Above all, in the way we live, we must not bring sorrow to the Holy Spirit who lives inside us. We must love and forgive others just as God through Jesus has loved and forgiven us.

FRI 1 AUG

97

CHALLENGE

Since becoming a Christian, have you slipped back, mixing a little bit of the world in with your Christian faith? Are their things you're currently doing that are compromising your faith and upsetting God? Take a moment to think, pray and ask God for a clean start today.

KEY VERSE
v14

'For all who are led by the Spirit of God are children of God.'

We're just about to start our final week exploring the subject of 'Living'. For the next few days, we're back with Paul's letter to the Romans, looking at how to live out a godly life.

It's reassuring to know that once we've given our life to Jesus and chosen to follow Him daily, we are completely made clean in God's sight. Even though none of us are perfect in this life, and make mistakes from time to time, God still loves us and is so proud to call us His children. In fact – as chapter 8 begins – there is now 'no condemnation for those who belong to Christ Jesus'. The Holy Spirit has freed us from the power of sin that leads to death. So, although we'll all stop 'living' this earthly life one day, death has no power over us, because we'll carry on living in the next life with God. Amazing! (See also v.10.)

So, in the light of this wonderful truth, Paul tells his friends in Rome about what God has done for them in Jesus and explains that those who don't know God personally are still controlled by the old sinful nature.

In verses 9–14, Paul explains that we are no longer slaves to this old nature. We don't have to obey it. Jesus has conquered it and we now have God's Spirit living in us, teaching us to live right. Imagine that – God's very own Spirit living in YOU! As God's children, we are now led by His Spirit.

PRAY

Father, if I stop and think about it for a moment, it truly is amazing that You have made Your home in me – that Your Spirit now lives in me and leads me into all truth. Lord God, teach me to live a life that pleases You. Help me not to fall back into the old nature of repeated sin. Give me the strength, by Your Spirit, to overcome temptation and to work at loving and serving others for Your glory.

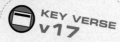
'So I am not the one doing wrong; it is sin living in me that does it.'

KEY VERSE v17

MON 4 AUG

100

THINK

Be assured today that you have God's Spirit to help you live and to help you say sorry when you mess up due to the sinful nature still battling against you this side of heaven! None of us will be perfect until we finally get to heaven – where there'll be no more sin!

Ever felt the way Paul describes in this passage? You want so desperately to do the right thing by God but you end up sinning! Don't worry – Paul has the answer because he recognises that in our earthly Christian lives there's always going to be a battle between God's way and sin's way.

The end result is already safe – we are saved eternally by Jesus' death on the cross. However, we still have to live out our lives here on earth in a world that is full of sinners and with our own fallen humanity that so desires sin. There's a spiritual battle going on!

In verse 24, Paul poses the question, 'Who will free me from this life that is dominated by sin and death?' Of course, we know Paul has the answer; he goes on to finish the passage by saying: 'The answer is in Jesus Christ our Lord. So you see how it is: In my mind I really want to obey God's law, but because of my sinful nature I am a slave to sin.' Remember, we have the Spirit of God to show us how to live even when sin still battles to control our way of living.

KEY VERSE
v2

'Think about the things of heaven, not the things of earth.'

So how do we start battling against the 'old nature' of sin that Paul described in Romans? Today we'll find out by looking at Paul's letter to his friends in Colosse.

Paul challenged them – and us in the fast-paced twenty-first century – to think about the things of heaven not of earth. What does he mean? You might think, 'I've got friends and family, my future career and money to think about.' Paul isn't saying you should spend all your time with your head in the clouds, hoping that things will turn out all right in the end. Later in the chapter you'll see Paul gives practical guidelines about how to live on earth.

In verses 5–9, Paul is also straight down the line about how *not* to live. He lists the characteristics of worldly living and in verse 10 he challenges us to put on our 'new nature' as Christians and live to get to know our Creator.

As we live in this new nature we can take a healthy approach to matters that still concern us on earth – family, friends, careers and money – viewing all matters through the lens of a heavenly perspective.

TUES 5 AUG

101

CHALLENGE

Is there something in your life you need to say sorry to God for today? Do it! How are you going to start thinking about the things of heaven? Why not start by reading the next part of Colossians 3, to verse 17, and then think about how you can treat those you know in this way?

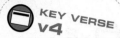

'Always be full of joy in the Lord. I say it again – rejoice!'

KEY VERSE v4

WED 6 AUG

102

We've seen this week how Paul identified the spiritual battle we face in ourselves, to resist the 'old nature' of sin and embrace the 'new nature' of God's Holy Spirit. Through reading some of Colossians, we've also looked at keeping our minds on heavenly not earthly things. So how, as we go about living for God, can we remain content with our own lives in a painful world that's always trying to make us feel discontented?

Paul tells us to always be full of joy in God. Is he mad? Bad things happen that upset us! Surely we're not supposed to be full of joy if a friend dies or a relative falls seriously ill, are we? This isn't what Paul is saying. Let's remember that Paul, as a result of following Jesus, had been whipped, stoned, thrown in jail, shipwrecked more than once, left cold and hungry and bad-mouthed by fellow Christians in his efforts to spread the good news. If he is a man who says we have something to rejoice about, rejoice!

The truth is, we rejoice because our future destiny is eternal life with God, and the hope that is now in us can help get through life's hard times!

PRAY

Father, I realise that this world is not perfect; that people suffer, that I've suffered and that bad things happen to good people. Lord, help me to be content in life and choose to receive Your joy as I fix my eyes on the hope of eternal life.

KEY VERSE v3

'Don't be selfish; don't try to impress others. Be humble, thinking of others as better than yourselves.'

Let's look at some further encouragement Paul gave the Philippians. In verses 1 and 2, Paul is simply saying, 'If you're just the slightest bit happy about knowing Jesus [when really he knows they have been absolutely transformed] then make me happy by continuing to live for God.'

Then Paul gets practical and tells them how to live: 'Don't be selfish! Stay humble! Consider others as better than you! Don't just look out for your own interests, but also look out for other people's welfare!' This kind of teaching flies right in the face of what the world says to us about 'looking after number one ... grabbing what you can ... making sure you're OK'.

Paul then tells his friends to model their attitudes on that of Jesus, highlighting the amazing humility God showed in giving up His position in heaven, squeezing His eternal being into the form of a man, and then dying for us.

Finally, Paul urges us to serve people without complaining or grumbling, so that nobody can criticise us as we live out pure lives as children of God in a very sinful, ungodly world.

THURS 7 AUG

103

THINK

When was the last time you did something without complaining or grumbling? When was the last time you thought of others as better than yourself – not by putting yourself down but by respecting them more? Have you been actively looking out for the interests of others recently?

'Teacher, which is the most important commandment in the law of Moses?'

KEY VERSE
v36

We've come to the end of our two-part series on 'Living', examining, among other things, the book of Ecclesiastes and Paul's letters to several churches.

Today, we sum up all that it means to live for God and celebrate life. Let's look at Jesus' reply to the very sneaky question highlighted in our key verse. This question was from an expert in Jewish Law (a Pharisee), who was trying to discredit Jesus' teachings.

Jesus responded with two statements. The first, in verse 37, affirmed the *Shema*, an important Jewish prayer taken from the words of Moses. Loving God with all your heart, soul, mind and strength was no problem for the Pharisees who recited the Shema twice a day. When another expert in the Law asked Jesus about the statement in verse 39, 'Love your neighbor as yourself', the reply Jesus gave would have been revolutionary to his thinking. The Pharisees loved themselves and their religion, but weren't concerned with the welfare of others.

PRAY

Father, help me to embrace Jesus' teaching on the two greatest commandments. I want to love You with everything I've got. Help me to do that. And, as I do, help me to love others and be concerned with their needs, just as I am with my own.

KEY VERSE v9

'Then the LORD God called to the man, "Where are you?"'

OBEYING

Welcome back to the challenging subject of *Obeying*. Let's look at the very first time human beings disobeyed God. This happened after the creation of the world and is commonly referred to as 'the Fall'.

We are told that the serpent (the devil) was shrewder than any of the wild animals the Lord had made. He tempts Eve by questioning God's original instructions: 'Did God *really* say ...?' (my italics). Then, the devil goes on to suggest to her that God was out to spoil their fun (vv.3–5). Finally, he convinces Eve that God is worried that she will become like Him: '... you will be like God, knowing both good and evil' (v.5).

CONTINUED ▸▸

The end result of Satan's plan is Eve and Adam's eventual disobedience and breaking of God's rules. Of all the trees in the Garden of Eden, there was one from which they were forbidden to eat (see Gen. 2:16–17), yet God had originally created human beings with the ability to choose what they wanted to do. We can choose to follow God or choose to go our own way.

Free will still exists today within every human being. We all have the ability to steal, lie, kill and murder, yet we also have the ability to cry out in praise and live to worship the Lord of heaven and earth. What will you choose today? How will you live your life – in obedience or disobedience?

CHALLENGE

When are you tempted? What areas of life do you struggle with? Where does your will and God's will collide? Spend some time thinking things through and, if you need to get right with God by saying sorry, use this moment to pray to Him and receive His gift of forgiveness and a clean start.

'"Where is your brother? Where is Abel?" "I don't know," Cain responded. "Am I my brother's guardian?"'

Shortly after the Fall, Adam and Eve have two sons, Cain and Abel. One son later dies – not through severe famine or even disease. He is murdered. This leaves only a handful of people on the planet. Let's look at the story of those two brothers: Cain and Abel.

Cain is the firstborn of Adam and Eve, and is a farmer, growing crops on the land. Abel is the second son and is a shepherd. At harvest time, Abel brings a generous portion from his flock to sacrifice to God, yet Cain brings only *some* of his fruits. The difference between 'the *best* of the firstborn lambs from his flock and *some* of his crops represents the difference in attitude towards worship of these two brothers.

God is pleased with Abel's choice generous portion but not with Cain's portion. Cain is filled with anger and jealousy, and later murders his brother out in the fields. Sadly, Cain's disobedience in not doing what was right by God has disastrous consequences; not only for Abel, but for the rest of Cain's life on earth.

MON 11 AUG

107

Father, I find it hard to obey Your ways sometimes. Please help me, though, to learn to obey Your rules for living and to trust that they are the right ways to lead my life, even when I don't feel like obeying!

PRAY

'The LORD has prevented me from having children. Go and sleep with my servant. Perhaps I can have children through her.'

KEY VERSE
v2

THINK

TUES 12 AUG

108

Surely, if God is God and He always keeps His promises, then it's far better for us to trust in Him than to take matters into our own hands? We're only human and prone to messing things up! God is not human and everything He does is brilliant and has perfect timing. Trust in God!

In our two previous studies, disobedience has focused on *not* doing the right thing (eating forbidden fruit and giving a poor offering). Now we see Abram bowing to pressure from Sarai, his wife, and trying to fix things himself, without bothering to consult God. He takes matters into his own hands to try to solve their problems – over which they have no control in the first place!

God had promised Abram that he would be the father of a great nation (Gen. 12:2-3) but both he and Sarai were getting very old and time was running out. They were still childless. Sarai suggests that Abram has children through Hagar, her Egyptian maidservant. Abram disobeys God – by trying to fix the problem himself rather than trusting in God's original promise. The result of this disobedience is the birth of a son, Ishmael, who grows up to be in conflict with all his relatives.

Do you try to fix problems yourself? Do you trust God with your relationships, your life and your future, or do you want to control your own destiny? Are you obeying and trusting God's promises today?

KEY VERSE
v10

'And Abraham picked up the knife to kill his son as a sacrifice.'

Yesterday's disobedient Abraham is (today) the perfect example of obedience. Earlier, Abram had neither trusted God for his own safety, deceiving Pharaoh over his true relationship with Sarai (Gen. 12:10–20), nor trusted God to provide them with a son (Gen. 16:1–4). Now we see him completely trusting and depending on God – who was asking him to give up his son, Isaac. Abraham agrees, taking Isaac to the mountain to sacrifice him. He trusts God to raise Isaac again from the dead (Heb. 11:17–19), telling his servants: 'We [Abraham and Isaac] will worship there, and then we will come right back' (v.5).

In pagan religions at the time humans were often sacrificed to appease the gods, but the Bible tells us clearly that God hates child sacrifice – so at the least it was a very unusual command to Abraham. As Abraham climbed the mountain, God was testing him to see how obedient he'd become. As he prepared to sacrifice Isaac, God noted Abraham's obedience and supplied a ram as an alternative – to take Isaac's place.

Through this, Abraham learned to trust God with his most precious possession (Isaac) – he was willing to give up everything to obey God. In following God, Abraham had learnt to develop faith, obedience and trust.

Thank You, Lord, for the example of Abraham. May I learn to trust and obey You as completely in all areas of my life.

WED 13 AUG

109

PRAY

'It's Esau, your firstborn son. I've done as you told me ... Now sit up and eat it so you can give me your blessing.'

KEY VERSE
v19

THURS 14 AUG

THINK

Do you have your entire life planned out? Is there space for God? Spend some time praying to God who knows how to give good gifts. Allow Him to speak to you about His plans for your life. Allow Him to begin to shape your destiny as you live to obey His will.

The Bible is full of stories of people who are disobedient. Esau is the first-born son of Isaac and the rightful heir of the family's wealth. Jacob (meaning deceiver) is the second-born and deserves a lesser inheritance.

Through scheming with his mother, Rebekah, Jacob deceives his father and steals Esau's birthright. Jacob then goes on the run from his brother, fearing never to be able to return home again. Through a combination of deceit, disguise and theft, Jacob gains what he's longed for but loses everything he had – all through disobedience.

God has our best intentions at heart. Jesus called Him a kind Father, who gives us what we need: 'You fathers – if your children ask for a fish, do you give them a snake instead? ... So if you sinful people know how to give good gifts to your children, how much more will your heavenly Father give the Holy Spirit ...' (Luke 11:11,13).

We always think we know best and, like disobedient children, we often wander off into trouble and strife. As with Jacob, our disobedient actions can cause long-lasting rifts with friends and family members.

KEY VERSE v1

'Children, obey your parents because you belong to the Lord, for this is the right thing to do.'

The first four of the Ten Commandments are based on our relationship with a God who loves us and wants us to obey Him. We now look at the laws that are given to ensure that society can live together, without anarchy and disunity.

The building block for society is the family unit. From our parents we learn respect, love, duty and responsibility. It is these lessons that teach us how to be productive and law-abiding citizens. By abiding by the rules of your parents, you learn to abide by the laws of society. And just as we see the growing breakdown of the family unit through divorce and separation, we also see in society an increase of crime, violence and robbery.

In his letter to the believers in Ephesus, Paul is echoing the fifth commandment Moses gave to the Hebrews, as recorded in Exodus 20 and Deuteronomy 5. He is explaining how it still applies to them even after they, as Jews, have decided to follow Jesus.

As hard as it may be, the honour and respect we pay our parents ultimately show our love for God and our obedience to His commands.

FRI 15 AUG

111

PRAY

Lord, please help me always to honour my parents and, whilst I live with them, to respect their opinions and live by their rules, as long as they don't compromise my faith in You.

KEY VERSE
v15

'Anyone who hates another brother or sister is really a murderer at heart.'

The greatest of God's creation – made in His image – are human beings, and His greatest gift to humanity is the very life He breathed into our nostrils on the sixth day of creation. To take that life from someone is murder. God gave Moses and the Hebrews the sixth commandment: 'You must not murder' (Exod. 20:13).

I would guess that very few of you are actually murderers. Society frowns upon murder: it is the worst crime of all to take someone's life. It carries severe punishment for those found guilty.

However, in today's key verse from 1 John, we read a very controversial statement. Are we *really* murderers if we hate someone? In Mark 7:14–23, when Jesus was teaching His disciples about purity, He was correcting the religious teaching of the Pharisees who taught people about avoiding certain types of food because the foods made them impure if they ate them. Jesus taught that we become sinful and impure when we allow ourselves to re-enact in our minds, think about or speak of hurting, injuring or hating another person.

Our mind, if left to wander, has the potential to become full of sinful thoughts about how we could hurt, get even with or beat up someone. These thoughts are wrong, and have the potential to develop into actual crimes, maybe even murder. We must take our thought life to Jesus every day, to be cleaned up by His forgiving power.

CHALLENGE

Take some time out to ask God to forgive you for the thoughts that have not been pure and have not brought glory to Him. Ask God to help you with these thoughts in the future and to give you ways of focusing on things that are pure.

'But I say, anyone who even looks at a woman with lust has already committed adultery with her in his heart.'

KEY VERSE v28

MON 18 AUG

114

THINK

Many of us would never commit the actual act of adultery, but this is a hard commandment to obey in our minds. Examine your thought life? Are you obeying this commandment? Are you watching or reading material you shouldn't be?

God's perfect plan was for one man and one woman to stay together forever. Within that plan there would be trust, encouragement, love and the gift of healthy sex. However, in today's world, sex sells – everything from perfume to cars. Our natural, God-given physiological desire for re-creation (our 'sex drive') has been exploited by the media – into a multi-million pound industry.

Adultery means sex between two people not married to each other – when at least one of them is already legally married to someone else (eg a married individual sleeping with an unmarried person, or two married people cheating on their husband or wife). The enormous repercussions of adultery don't just affect the two people involved, but can destroy family relationships and friendships.

Jesus expands the seventh commandment – *You must not commit adultery* – to include also the mental aspect of adultery. If left unchecked, our mind can entertain lustful thoughts towards other people's girlfriends/ boyfriends, husbands/wives or even married film stars or pop stars – and Jesus warns us that this too is a kind of adultery.

'You must not steal.'

Today we examine the eighth commandment: 'You must not steal.'

Cartoons often portray the typical thief in a black-and-white-striped shirt, face mask and a sack, marked with the word 'Swag'. However, there are more ways to steal than holding up a bank, mugging an OAP or breaking into a car. All of us are probably guilty of having stolen something at least once in our lives.

You may not be involved in serious crime, but do you steal time from your employer by knocking off early or helping yourself to items in the stationery cupboard? Do you 'borrow' from friends without ever really considering paying them back? Do we give to God our time, money or energy, or do we steal time from Him by only having a one-sided relationship with Him – calling on Him only in times of emergency?

None of these 'crimes', of course, are likely to get us locked up, but they are still stealing. Think through your lifestyle: the attitude you adopt when you borrow from parents and friends; the way you work for your employer. Are you stealing? Are you obeying God's commandment not to steal?

TUES 19 AUG

115

THINK

Think through your actions. Do you have things that belong to other people which you have 'borrowed' or actually stolen from them? How many of your MP3s have you paid for recently? Were they 'file shared'? Could you be stealing from record companies?

'Many false witnesses spoke against him, but they contradicted each other.'

KEY VERSE v56

PRAY

Father, I want to live differently to people who don't know You. When I speak, I want to speak truth about my neighbour, about situations and about my actions. Help me to live a life of truth, under the inspiration of Your Holy Spirit living in me.

When Jesus was brought before the high priest, many spoke against Him, making up stories that simply weren't true. They lied and broke the ninth commandment, trying to get Jesus murdered.

The term 'white lie' is an interesting idea. Sometimes we lie to avoid upsetting people, *'Oh, yes, that dress really suits you!'* or to avoid punishment, *'My computer disk crashed and I lost all my work, Sir!'*

We use lots of alternative words to describe lying: *duplicity, fabrication, evasion, stringing someone along, inaccuracy, exaggeration, fudging, rationalisation, falsehood, 'whopper', deception, misrepresentation, dishonesty, putting on a mask,* and *fibbing.* However, at the end of the day, lies are lies!

When we lie about other people, we do them a great injustice and we break God's ninth commandment. With one false word or sentence, we can set someone else's life on a totally different course – maybe even send them to prison! This is what the false witnesses tried to do to Jesus – but they couldn't get their stories straight. Jesus was a totally innocent Man.

KEY VERSE
v17

'You must not covet your neighbor's house ... or anything else that belongs to your neighbor.'

Most of the commandments we've examined in the second part of our study of *Obeying* relate to our actions: *lying, stealing, killing, committing adultery*. However, this next commandment deals with the heart attitude of the believer. It exposes and convicts our internal thought lives. Are we jealous of someone? Are we envious of someone else's material possessions? Are we greedy for more? The human heart is unseen to fellow Christians but is always seen by God.

When we look at the word 'house' within this commandment, does it deal with more than just bricks and mortar? Could it also be the contents of a neighbour's house – material possessions we envy? Maybe it could be relationships that we envy? We may even have adulterous thoughts or feelings ...

If all of society obeyed God's tenth commandment, public crime would cease. Houses would be left unlocked and mobile phones wouldn't need to have their SIMs blocked – as they wouldn't be stolen! Are there things that your friends have that you're wrongly jealous of? Or have you, like Paul (Phil. 4:12), learned to be content with what you have?

THURS 21 AUG

117

THINK

God wants to do some open-heart surgery on you today. Psalm 139:1 tells us that God has 'examined' our heart and knows 'everything' about us! He knows the things we long for and desire, and wants to free us from impure longings (coveting) for things that aren't ours.

'For my yoke is easy to bear, and the burden I give you is light.'

KEY VERSE v30

PRAY

Father, teach me to obey and to accept the rules You've laid down on how to live life – and therefore live it to the full!

We've come to the end of our study on *Obeying*. We've looked at how characters in the Bible like Abraham, Jacob and Daniel obeyed (or disobeyed) God. We've even examined how Jesus obeyed the Father. And we've also explored the Ten Commandments in detail, looking at how they still apply to our lives today.

So, are you feeling better about obeying? Sometimes it feels hard to obey, whilst at others it feels a pleasure to know that you are doing the right thing. It's even easy at times!

When Jesus spoke to the crowds He gave them the opportunity to receive His teaching and to follow His way of living; to follow and obey Him, and to lead a rich and fulfilling life. Jesus talked about bearing a yoke. Not an egg yolk, but the yoke (or wooden crosspiece that attached two oxen together at the neck) used to harness animals to pull farm machinery. Jesus describes Himself as one of these oxen and we have the opportunity of being His partner. We can take on a light (not a heavy or religious) yoke of obedience to live out a life of faith – doing the work of heaven on earth.

Are you ready to be yoked to Christ? Will you obey Him in everything?

KEY VERSE
v3

'Go back to what you heard and believed at first; hold to it firmly.'

END TIMES

Welcome back to the third and final instalment of what the Bible has to say regarding the End Times. In this final section we'll look at how the End Times impact our lives personally and how we can live in the assurance of eternal life.

As we saw in the last section, the most important point that Jesus made about the 'End Times' was the

CONTINUED ▶▶

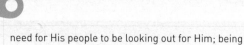

need for His people to be looking out for Him; being ready and waiting.

This life has many distractions that can turn our attention away from living the Christian life. We can lose our way and become exposed to bad habits, or give into peer pressure and believe lies that weaken our relationship with Jesus.

Like a computer that searches for online updates from the software and security providers, we need to regularly evaluate our lives to make sure that we've 'downloaded' the 'Holy Spirit updates' required in order to function at our best as Christians. In this way we're protected from those things that would continue to weaken and erode our relationship with Jesus. If in doubt, the Bible says, go back to what you first believed and hold to it firmly!

CHALLENGE

If there's something you would like to get sorted with God before Jesus returns, then now's the opportunity. Each day this week ask the Holy Spirit to help you with it and think about what you can do practically to change or overcome in this area of your life.

KEY VERSE
v2

'Five of them were foolish, and five were wise.'

Today's passage really relates to the classic Scout and Guide motto – 'Be prepared'. Some of us find this motto a little too cheesy, but unfortunately we can't escape the truth behind this parable. However, it's what we do about it that counts.

If we're going to be ready for Jesus' return, we need to ensure that our lamps of faith are still burning brightly to welcome Him back. In this sense, the oil could be taken to represent all that strengthens our faith: anything from reading the Bible, sharing testimonies and God stories with your Christian mates, to listening to Christian rock music on your MP3 player or helping others to find faith.

We can all burn out from time to time under the pressure of doubt, personal insecurity and suffering, so keeping full of the Holy Spirit is crucial in order to keep ourselves on fire for Jesus – even through the tough times! So whatever you like doing to strengthen your faith, do it as much as possible, so that you can be prepared for Christ's return – having enough fuel to keep your Christian fire burning.

MON 25 AUG

121

THINK

Is there something that you could add into your lifestyle that would strengthen your faith? Perhaps reading these *Mettle* notes is a good start and a helpful way of opening up the Bible to you.

'For the Scriptures say, "You must be holy because I am holy."'

KEY VERSE
v16

TUES 26 AUG

122

Sometimes the word 'holy' can seem like a scary word. We all know that we're far from holy, because we know we're not perfect. Nevertheless, holiness is something that the Bible talks about working towards, within the overall sense of our eternal life starting now. Let's look at it as a series of stages.

Stage One of holy living is recognising that another person gives you holiness. You cannot earn it! It's a gift. Jesus Himself purchased your holiness with His life. Through believing and accepting this truth, you then start on a journey of developing holiness.

Stage Two of holy living is realising that Jesus lives in you and is interested in your entire person.

Stage Three of holy living is choosing to reveal every aspect of yourself to Christ – including those bits you're not proud of.

Stage Four of holy living is allowing yourself to be changed by the Holy Spirit. This means getting rid of unhelpful habits, prideful independence and arrogance.

These stages help to overcome the fear 'holiness', whilst keeping our focus on Christ's return and our eternal future.

PRAY

Lord, help me please to see which areas of my life need to be touched by You and help me to be willing to live a holy life for You.

KEY VERSE v23

'Watch out! I have warned you about this ahead of time!'

The non-Christian world has always been fascinated by the mysteries of the future and has developed many ways of trying to predict what will happen. Tarot cards, horoscopes, crystal balls, 'old wives tales' and even mediums all claim to offer insight into a person's future.

People can often become obsessed with reading their own horoscope or visiting palm readers in an attempt to discover what will happen to them. Mostly it seems that the world is stuck between a desire to know what happens and a fear of knowing what might happen! People can become controlled by the fear of what might happen to them as they listen to false prophecies about their life.

As Christians we do not need to fear the future and neither do we need to know exactly what will happen to us. If we belong to Christ, it's enough for us to know that He has the plan for our lives and will guide us by His Holy Spirit, according to this plan.

If you're someone who's been tempted by the desire to know the future, then turn to the Lord and trust Him for your life.

WED 27 AUG

123

Father, please help me to trust You for my future and protect me from situations where my faith might be compromised by the temptation to take the future into my own hands. Help me to keep away from spiritually harmful human methods of reading into the future.

PRAY

'And the one sitting on the throne said, "Look, I am making everything new!"'

KEY VERSE v5

THURS 28 AUG

THINK

Think of one thing you can do to help look after the planet. Look at the Tearfund or Christian Aid websites or visit www.christian-ecology.org.uk for recent information and ideas.

Question: *If God is busy making everything new, why do we need to bother about looking after the world we live in?*

It's a good question, and one requiring a careful answer. It would be easy for us to ignore issues such as climate change if we believe that Jesus could arrive in a few years' time, but we would also be ignoring the responsibility God gave humankind for the whole earth – not just for its inhabitants.

God didn't say to Adam and Eve, *'Just rule over all the humans'*. He gave them the task of ruling over *all* of creation. This being the case, we need to do our best to look after this planet – whether that's through recycling, starting a compost bin or choosing to have a holiday in the UK rather than flying around the world. This all helps to uphold our responsibility to look after that which God has entrusted to us. Whilst we don't need to become obsessed or start chaining ourselves to trees, it's good to remember that this planet cannot be taken for granted. Moreover, God will not forget what you do to look after what He has made.

KEY VERSE
4:18

'So we don't look at the troubles we can see now; rather, we fix our gaze on things that cannot be seen.'

Whilst there is so much about the End Times that is still a mystery to us, it's passages like today's that provide such a deep reassurance about where we are all heading as Christians.

The thought of being given a new body so full of life that it totally swallows up the old one is just incredible. It provides us with great hope for the future. We might not be able to see the detail of what lies ahead for humanity, but we do know what God has planned for us as His children: an amazing, perfect and joyful relationship with Him, free from the sin and pain of this life. We can be confident that God will continue the relationship that He first started with humanity in the Garden of Eden.

In the meantime, we must recognise the need to keep our eyes fixed on Him and not upon the troubles and stresses that this life brings, which can easily eclipse our view of God. With Jesus as the focal point in our lives, we will always be able to keep placing one foot in front of the other along the journey of this life and into the next.

FRI 29 AUG

125

PRAY

Father, I give over to You the things that have been troubling me. I ask You to become my focal point, so that I can keep putting one foot in front of the other this week and live out my Christian faith amongst my family and friends.

KEY VERSE
v12

'If we endure hardship, we will reign with him.'

We've covered a lot whilst looking at the End Times and I hope that you have been inspired and encouraged about all that is still to come. We've considered some teaching about what the End Times are, what Jesus said about them and finally what the impact of the End Times is for our lives now.

The last thing that stands out about the End Times is the way in which all of us have to endure to the end, regardless of whether that end is death or the return of Jesus in our lifetime. Living with the expectation that He could return soon is something that helps us to endure life's hard times. It's encouraging to know that there *will* be an end to all the pain and suffering.

Our challenge is to keep going and to overcome sin, so that one day we might reign with Christ over the earth, sharing with Him in His glory. When we're thinking about our response to the End Times, we just have to remember to be ready, holy and patient, continuing to fulfil God's purpose for our lives and maintaining our focus on our Lord Jesus, who will return one day to finally bring an end to sin and death.

CHALLENGE

Skim through the Mettle notes on the End Times again. Was there anything that stood out for you or anything that you didn't quite understand? If so, talk about these things with someone you trust. Don't be afraid to ask for further explanation!

ORDER FORM

4 EASY WAYS TO ORDER:

1. For credit/debit card payment, call 01252 784710 (Mon–Fri, 9.30am–5pm)

2. Visit our Online Store at www.cwrstore.org.uk

3. Send this form together with a cheque made payable to CWR to: CWR, Waverley Abbey House, Waverley Lane, Farnham, Surrey GU9 8EP

4. Visit your local Christian bookshop

YOUR DETAILS

Name:

CWR ID No. (if known):

Address:

Postcode:

Telephone No. (for queries):

Email:

SUBSCRIPTIONS° (NON DIRECT DEBIT)	QTY	PRICE (INCLUDING P&P)			TOTAL
		UK	Europe	Elsewhere	
Mettle (1yr, 3 issues)		£11.50	£13.50	Please contact nearest National Distributor or CWR direct*	
				TOTAL **B**	

(Subscription prices already include postage and packing)

Please circle which four-monthly issue you would like your subscription to commence from:

JAN–APR   **MAY–AUG**   **SEP–DEC**

*For a list of our National Distributors, who supply countries outside the UK, visit www.cwr.org.uk/distributors